Is there anything in the corner?

A Journey in Discovering God's Faithfulness

TAMI O'NEAL

ISBN 979-8-89130-434-5 (paperback)
ISBN 979-8-89130-435-2 (digital)

Copyright © 2024 by Tami O'Neal

All rights reserved. No part of this publication may be reproduced, distributed, or transmitted in any form or by any means, including photocopying, recording, or other electronic or mechanical methods without the prior written permission of the publisher. For permission requests, solicit the publisher via the address below.

Christian Faith Publishing
832 Park Avenue
Meadville, PA 16335
www.christianfaithpublishing.com

Printed in the United States of America

*For Kyle, Eden, and Maverick who have held my
hands and stood by me throughout this project.
May we always face life together with
confidence as Team O'Neal.
And for my parents who love me no matter what.*

This is my story; this is my song:
Praising my Saviour all the day long.
Blessed Assurance

—Fanny Crosby, 1873

Contents

Preface		vi
Introduction		viii
One	Halo-Halo	1
Two	The Three *B*s: "Bath, Potty, and Bed"	17
Three	Banana Prayers	29
Four	Stage Fright	45
Five	Roots	62
Six	Wings	77
Seven	Night Flight	96
Eight	~~Failure~~ Restoration	111
Nine	Family Conflab	129
Ten	The Great Belladonna Took	141
Eleven	Texas Heat	155
Twelve	Adventure Is Out There!	168
Thirteen	What the Locusts Ate	185
Fourteen	To Run and Not Grow Weary	201
Photos		215
Acknowledgments		230
Bibliography		233

Preface

I have always felt that the written word provided clarity—a way of expressing oneself in a manner that was paradoxically logical, but also heartfelt. Once on paper, an element of sincerity presented itself; factual or not, words printed, like words spoken, could not be taken back.

I can remember, as a little girl, writing short stories about glamorous and adventurous characters with names so much more intriguing and mysterious than my own. Samantha, Caroline, Theresa, and Cynthia were who my seven-year-old romanticist longed to be. Hiding under my bed, I scribbled their stories out on scraps of paper as fast as I could make my pencil form the letters. I was confident that these characters and their tales of heroism were so gripping that I needed to write them down in secret in case someone else committed them to paper before I could. Later, my longing to put my thoughts on paper was a means of bringing to life my deepest desires that lay in turmoil within me. If I could see my heart on paper, formed into words, perhaps others would understand what I couldn't bring myself to say out loud.

And so, I have always had an interest in writing: to write what I feel, share what I have learned and discovered, and explain the reasons I am the way I am, in an attempt to relate to others. As I approach middle age, my desire to write has shifted away from the need to explain myself and who I am to the desire to share what God has done for me. His redemptive work in my life is the only explanation that really matters. For my readers, and particularly for my own children, my desire is for you to know "how wide, how long, how high, and how deep is the love of God" (Ephesians 3:18b NLT).

I pray that the words committed to paper here are words of encouragement and hope. I pray that the anecdotal happenings of my life recorded here may point you, the reader, to Christ. And ultimately, may His life-giving words restore and redeem all who hear them.

Introduction

"Is there anything in the corner?" Each night before I climbed up into my platform bed made of plywood and rolled under the mosquito net, I would ask my parents to check the dark corner where the end of my bed met the end of my sister's bed. Our beds lay in an L shape against the walls of our one-room grass house. The corner post of our house where our beds touched was a tree trunk. There was always some type of insect that managed to make this tree trunk post its home. I knew this for two reasons. The first reason was that the bark had been removed from the tree trunk, and I could see the holes it had created as it burrowed into the wood. The second reason was that whatever insect had decided to call this wood post home had also decided to create a mess on my bed by leaving its droppings there. This corner was nearly always hidden in darkness.

The Coleman kerosene lantern that hung from the wooden rafters was the only source of light after the sun set. The lantern, hung by a set of rope pulleys that allowed it to be lowered and raised, was set at the perfect height—low enough that it did not set the thatched grass roof ablaze and high enough that my parents could walk perfectly underneath it. The light from the lantern cast strange, shadowy shapes on the walls, especially when my dad didn't quite raise it high enough and failed to duck under it, hitting his head and sending the Coleman and the shadows spinning. My dad eventually found a better location for the Coleman lantern—one that posed less of a threat to his head!

We were a missionary family. For large portions of the year, we lived on a volcanic island called Babuyan Claro, located in the northern part of the Philippines. Because we lived in a small grass house with a thatched cogon grass roof, it is a miracle that we never set our house on fire in all the years we lived in it. Later, the grass walls were replaced by wooden planks, but that didn't seem to reduce the potential for our house to turn into a bonfire if we were careless. You can imagine my concern as I got ready for bed each night. What type of little creature might have crawled in through the cracks in the wood walls?

I had a very clear picture of what needed to take place at bedtime before I could feel secure enough in my netted haven to fall asleep. Each night, I felt it was my parents' duty to check the dark corner for anything—anything at all that might be hiding there in the darkness. Thus, each night, my parents had the supreme pleasure of inspecting the dark corner to reassure me (and sometimes my sister) that there was indeed nothing there. They would then proceed to meticulously tuck the ends of my mosquito net tightly under the thin mattress, ensuring that nothing could make its way into my safe zone. The tucking in of the net was so paramount to my safety that it did not occur to me that if something were already inside my sweet little bulwark, it would have no way out!

My parents tell me I was around age four or five the night the centipede bit me. I woke up in the blackness of the night crying, saying that something had stung me. After dismantling my bed and finding nothing, I was told to go back to sleep. In the morning, I had a red and swollen throbbing hand. A large centipede was found flattened beneath my mattress.

The idea that something might be in the corner in the unchartered shadowland where my imagination can run rampant has chased me throughout my life. My childhood questions of *Is there?* and *What if?* gradually turned into *How come?* and *Why me?* as I grew into adulthood. My longing for answers, for resolution, for security, for strength to overcome my struggles continue to tug at my heart. But despite my questions, I know that I am not alone. There is a still, quiet reassurance, a beam of light in the darkness, the Word of Truth whispering life into my soul. "'My grace is all you need. My power works best in weakness.' So now I am glad to boast about my weaknesses, so that the power of Christ can work through me."[1]

---

[1] 2 Corinthians 12:9 (NLT).

One

Halo-Halo

*I praise you because I am fearfully
and wonderfully made.*

Psalm 139:14

I have lived with the tension of the in-between my whole life, a blending of worlds in a collision of cultures. The act of balancing languages and cultures, countries and continents, was in many ways as natural to my family as grocery shopping. A little bit of this and a little bit of that, and somehow, the cart is full to the brim with everything necessary to survive the next week.

The Filipinos have a fantastic word to describe this: *halo-halo* (haa-low haa-low). *Halo-halo*, meaning *mixed*, is actually a somewhat random edible concoction highly favored by Filipinos. *Halo-halo* consists of shaved ice, evaporated milk or condensed milk, shredded young coconut, sweetened red beans, toasted rice that had previously been pounded flat (called *pinipig*), boiled cubes of yam, pieces of fruit, *nata de coco*, flan, and *ube* ice cream (purple ice cream where the purple *ube* yam is the main ingredient). The rich, deep-purple color of the *ube* ice cream draws your eye and creates an explosion of flavor in your mouth. *Halo-halo* can contain all or some of these ingredients or as many combinations of these items as you might imagine. In essence, my life growing up was a blend of ingredients, stemming from my parents' upbringing—a perfect example of *halo-halo*.

My *halo-halo* life comes directly as a result of my parents' decision to become missionaries with Wycliffe Bible Translators. They traveled with their two little girls in tow, teaching them how to adapt and blend as they learned new languages and cultures, climates, and terrain. Those two little girls were my sister and me.

I am a mixture of sorts, blessed with dual citizenship from the United States and Canada, but born and raised in the Philippines as an MK/TCK (missionary kid / third-culture kid) to a Chinese American mother and a Rhodesian father. I spent my growing-up years learning French, Chinese, and various Filipino languages (all without much success or fluency, I might add). I was raised to believe that all cultures, all people, and all languages are loved by God (even if you speak them poorly like I do). "*There are many different languages in the world, and every language has meaning.*"[2] Living in the "in-between," I came to understand that distinction and diversity are truly a picture of God's creativity and artistry. *Halo-halo* at its best!

Daughter of Chinese immigrants, my mother was born and raised in San Francisco, California. A first-generation ABC (American-born Chinese), my mother was no stranger to diversity. She lived in between worlds,

---

[2] 1 Corinthians 14:10 (NLT).

adapting and blending, just as she taught me to. As a latchkey kid, my mother wore her house key on a chain around her neck, going to and from elementary school on her own. After school, she would join the rest of her family at the *Gai Chong*[3] (sewing factory), clipping loose threads off bundles of freshly pressed pants before they were sent off to the dealers. Later, when she was a little older, she was promoted to the machines where she began the process of overlocking, making buttonholes, and eventually sewing pairs of pants from start to finish. She spoke English with her friends at school and with her siblings, but Toisanese, a dialect of Cantonese, at home with her parents, uncles, and aunts.

Gung Gung (maternal grandfather) spoke to me only in broken English, and *Pau Pau* (maternal grandmother) rattled off directions to me in Toisanese so fast that I typically only caught her meaning by gestures and an occasional "*Ai ya!*" or a toothy grin with a thumbs-up. On one visit, *Pau Pau* was eager to practice her new English vocabulary with my sister and me. She grinned proudly as she pointed to a bowl of fruit on the table and said, "*Ba-na-na*," and then threw her thumb up in the air!

Driving from the airport to their three-story apartment building on Blake Street, I can remember straining my neck to see if they would be sitting at the bay window waiting for our car to drive up. (They had purchased this

---

[3] All spellings of the words in Toisanese are indicative of how I remember my mother pronouncing and spelling them. Note that there are differences in spelling and pronunciation across the numerous Chinese dialects, and these may differ from ones that might be familiar to the reader. In addition, I have left off tone marks in the pinyin words that I borrowed from the Toisanese language.

apartment building years before after moving from North Beach.) Once we had climbed the hard, plastic-covered stairs to their apartment door on the second floor, I could hear the shuffling of *Gung Gung's* slipper-clad feet making his way to unbolt the lock. Later, *Gung Gung* would take us downstairs and around the block to the little corner store, where he let us pick out a huge bag of Lay's potato chips. We would shyly whisper our thank you, *"Aw-dieh, Gung Gung. Aw-dieh."* Later, we would sit on the couch, crunching potato chips and watching the cartoon *She-Ra: Princess of Power* while he read the Chinese paper and commented on the state of whatever stocks he had invested. *Pau Pau* would sometimes watch with us but would inevitably stand up, muttering a low *"Ai ya"* while she shook her head and made her way to the kitchen. Holding her back, she would rattle off in Toisanese what I could only imagine were disapproving comments about the lack of clothing the Princess of Power wore.

Pau Pau was a fabulous cook, something my mother inherited. While we watched TV, she would be busy cooking a feast for dinner. As we got older, she invited my sister and me to learn how to make wontons, chuckling at our misshapen dumplings as she gently placed them next to her perfectly fashioned ones.

I learned early on that the secret to making *Pau Pau* happy was to eat plenty of the food she prepared. *Pau Pau's* food was always delicious, but there is only so much rice and savory beef and bok choy, or chicken sautéed in a wok with so many delicious flavors that a small child can eat.

The idea of eating "family style" takes on a whole new meaning at a Chinese table. Each person reaches in with the serving end of their chopsticks, multiple times, selecting their preferred choice of food items to go with their bowl of rice. If this was not done enough, *Pau Pau* would fill your bowl for you. It was *Pau Pau's* responsibility to make sure no one in her home left the table hungry. As a result, the moment the last piece of meat or vegetable from your bowl was lifted up by your chopsticks, a new helping of whatever dish was closest to *Pau Pau* landed in your bowl. It always amazed me how her fingers, crooked from arthritis, could so quickly whip those chopsticks upside down to serve us a new portion of food and then just as nimbly flip them back around to eat from her own bowl.

After dinner, she would grab a handful of leftover rice and form the perfect little *gai doy* by squeezing the rice with her hand to make it look like a little doggie. I can remember her soft chuckle as she picked off the sticky rice kernels from her fingers and tossed the *gai doy* into our bowls. One of the few words I still remember in Toisanese is *bo la*. "I'm full!"

Gung Gung and *Pau Pau* were fairly forgiving of our flaws and peculiar non-Chinese ways, and I have some happy memories of our short visits to Blake Street. I can still see the grins on my grandparents' faces when we did something "un-Chinese" that made them laugh. I can remember the look on *Pau Pau's* face when our elbows stuck out too far when we held our rice bowls at the dinner table, and she would flap her arms, shake her head, and say, "*Ai ya!*" to let us know we had *mo lai mao,* bad manners. Later, my sister and I would crawl under the dining room table to pick up kernels of rice that were the result of our messy eating. Perhaps it was our messy table manners that led to the rice kernels under the table, but more likely, it was evidence of our apparent lack of skill at using chopsticks to eat rice!

I can still see the red plastic cups with tiny round handles that we drank piping hot oolong tea from. The handles were so small I could barely fit my two fingers through them, and I remember being afraid I would spill my tea. Even though *Pau Pau* filled those red plastic cups to the brim with hot tea, they never seemed to melt the thick plastic tablecloth. Sitting by the window with *Gung Gung* and *Pau Pau*, our silence threw a shadow of regret that I did not learn to speak Toisanese so I could have asked them what they saw in those few moments we spent together.

There are other things I remember about the times we spent together with *Gung Gung* and *Pau Pau* in their home. I remember the ceramic Buddha with all the smiling little ceramic children around him that sat on the shelf just below the family pictures. The Buddha statue, with its big rolling belly, always reminded me a little bit of Santa Claus, jolly and rosy, but without the big bag of presents. I recall my mother telling me about the conversations she had with her parents in Toisanese about her faith in Jesus and that God had prepared a beautiful place for those who believe in Him, only to leave wondering if the good news had fallen on rocky ground.[4] My mother's courage to share what was most important to her with her family still leaves me with a sense of admiration. I believe she can truly say, *"For I am not ashamed of the gospel for it is the power of Christ that brings salvation for everyone who believes."*[5]

---

[4] Matthew 13:20.
[5] Romans 1:16 (NIV).

At the age of sixteen, my mother placed her trust in Jesus Christ as her Savior. While in high school, a friend shared her new faith in Jesus with my mom, explaining what she had come to learn about Jesus and His love for her. Little did my mother know that her choice to follow Jesus would one day lead her to join Wycliffe Bible Translators and follow the Lord's call to live on a remote island in the Philippines!

My mother's tenacity has always impressed me, and her consistency in prayer is no exception. Her prayers are what has given her the strength to not only endure but also persist through difficult times. As talented and smart as my mother is, she could have picked any career leading to a life of ease. Instead, she chose a life full of adventure, following and trusting in Jesus, her Lord and Savior. She has indeed *"chosen what is better, and it will not be taken away from her."*[6]

My father's story begins on the other side of the world, in the country of Rhodesia (now known as Zimbabwe). He spent his early growing-up years on Tjumpani farm, the Penny-Maree family dairy farm near the town of Plumtree. As a small boy, one of his jobs was to feed the bantam chickens. His favorite jobs, however, were to help milk the cows in the dairy and most of all to wind the milk cream separator machine. Later, around the age of nine or ten, his family moved to the little town of Plumtree. At that time, during the late 1950s and early 1960s, Plumtree was inhabited by only about one hundred or so white Africans. The black Africans were native to the area and lived in their tribal villages. Each tribe lived separately on its own tribal land area.

---

[6] Luke 10:42 (NIV).

Growing up with the concept of apartheid, my father learned the meaning of distinction at a very young age: distinct tribes, distinct territories, distinct colors of skin. His father, my grandpa Viv, had served seven years in the Rhodesian army on the front lines in Malta and Italy during World War II. After the war, he returned to Rhodesia to marry his sweetheart, Joy, and began to raise his family. Enlisted in the Reserve Army, however, he was forced to continue fighting to protect the Rhodesian border from communist insurgency from the north. War and bloodshed were experiences he did not want for his only son or for his family. And so, the decision was made to leave Africa, the land of their birth and the land their ancestors had settled in the 1600s. It was a decision to leave their home and family and trade it all for a new life in a new country on a new continent. Because of government restrictions, they left the keys in the car, took what little money they could out of the bank, and boarded a ship bound for England.

Over several years, and because Rhodesia had been a crown colony, my father and his family were permitted to immigrate to Canada where they were eventually accepted as Canadian citizens. (My father's journey to citizenship is a long one and perhaps for another book. It involved a time after graduating from college in the United States when he had no citizenship in any country!) His family arrived on the shores of New Brunswick in the middle of winter and spent that year in a small basement apartment, picking potatoes to make a living. I truly believe what held my father's family together during that cold winter on the eastern coast of Canada was their devotion to one another and their love for the Lord Jesus.

Ever since I can remember, Granny Maree, my father's mother (whom we affectionately called Granny or Gran and later Great-Granny Joy Joy by the youngest generation of great-grandchildren), would pray for everyone in her family by name every day. If ever there was a prayer warrior, she was it. I can remember her telling my husband (fiancé at the time) that she had added him to her prayer list and prayed for him by name each day. What an impact that had on me, knowing that if she said she would pray for something, she meant it and would be praying to the Almighty God for His intervention. Gran was about five foot two inches tall, but what she lacked in height, she sure made up for in her prayers and her fiery red hair! Her constant conversations with God were something I remember even as a child. As she puttered around the kitchen, making tea or mixing up dough for scones, her rings spinning around her fingers, she spoke to the Lord as if He were standing there right beside her. "Lord, You know all things," she would say as she warmed the tea kettle and set out china mugs for us.

I loved sitting at her kitchen table listening to her tell stories of their life in Africa long ago. We would drink tea together and eat the scones or waffle cookies she had made previously or perhaps some fresh berries and cream. I never tired of the stories of how she met Grandpa and the yellow dress that she wore when he went off to fight in the war. When it was time to leave and I would gather my things and head toward the door, she would say, "Have you ever heard the story of how Dad was born?" Off came my shoes and purse, and I would sit down once again to hear my father's birth story and how the Lord had His hand on him even as an infant. You see, my dad was one of two other Rundell Maree boys in the family.

The other two, unfortunately, did not survive after having rheumatic fever and other ailments. They were both born in July. My dad, too, suffered from rheumatic fever as a child, but the Lord had other plans for his life. He was born on June 30.

My dad's life has been spared many times over his now seventy-plus years. As I think back to all the events he lived through, I am reminded of the apostle Paul and his list of sufferings.[7] While working construction in Canada, a building fell on his back, pinning him to the floor. He broke his back and collarbone a second time on Christmas Day 1994 when he jumped up to hang on a broken soccer goal that came crashing down on him, crushing his sternum, neck and back, nose, and cheekbones and severely lacerating his tongue.

In the early 1970s, when he and my mother had first moved to the Philippines, he was wrongly arrested for what was misunderstood as building an illegal airstrip on Babuyan Island (a small island in the northern Philippines) and taken to the municipal island of Calayan and put under house arrest. ("*I have...been in prison*").[8] The purpose of this airstrip was to allow the JAARS planes to not only fly in supplies to the island but also to our family. This was an island where he and my mother (and later my sister and I) would eventually live, get to know the people on the island as family, and one day complete the translation of the Word of God into the mother-tongue language of the Ibatan people. When JAARS airplanes were no longer able to fly to Babuyan Island, for many years, he (and my mother) spent count-

---

[7] 2 Corinthians 11:22-33 (NIV).
[8] 2 Corinthians 11:23b (NIV).

less hours on the open sea, traveling in the local outrigger open boats to and from the northern coast of the Philippines and Babuyan Claro Island ("*I spent a night and a day in the open sea*").[9]

My dad has lived in more than six different countries and has spent the majority of his adult life regularly traveling back and forth between three ("*I have been constantly on the move...in danger in the country, in danger at sea; and in danger from false believers*").[10] My dad is also no stranger to what Paul lists next, "*I have labored and toiled and have often gone without sleep; I have known hunger and thirst and have often gone without food. Besides everything else, I face daily the pressure of my concern for all the churches.*"[11]

I have never had the pleasure (or the desire, I might add) to start a church and preach from the pulpit, but my parents not only felt called to translate the Bible into the language of the Ibatan people, but they also facilitated Bible study groups, a choir, a medical clinic, a high school, and a long list of academic publications to help document the language and history of the Ibatan. I can only imagine the pressure of making sure the body of believers was maturing spiritually, especially when they were constantly traveling and working on other projects.

Just as Paul does not simply leave the reader with a list of his trials and disparaging moments, my dad has continually pressed forward, knowing that despite the trials he faced, he was being obedient to the Lord's call on his life. Paul closes chapter 11 with hope and a renewed focus. He doesn't dwell on his bravery or tenacity but

---

[9] 2 Corinthians 11:25b (NIV).
[10] 2 Corinthians 11:26 (NIV).
[11] 2 Corinthians 11:27–38 (NIV).

chooses a deliberate recalibrating to place all emphasis on God. *"If I must boast, I will boast of the things that show my weakness. The God and Father of the Lord Jesus, who is to be praised forever, knows that I am not lying."*[12] This reiterates Paul's utter and complete devotion to the Lord in the previous chapter[13] where he quotes Jeremiah 9:24, *"As the Scriptures say, 'If you want to boast, boast only about the Lord.'"*

From the time I can remember, my dad has preceded many of his statements with *"If it is the Lord's will."* As a family, we prayed together daily, read Scripture together daily, and planned for our future trips and events together. My dad would always remind us that while we could plan away to our hearts' content, we would eventually fail if we did not seek the Lord first, asking for His guidance, direction, and protection in our lives.[14] What we hoped to accomplish would only be possible because of the Lord. He would then remind us, when we did complete a task or accomplish a goal, to give thanks to God for answering our prayers and for giving us the ability to do what we had set out to do.

I have often wondered with amazement how a young girl from Chinatown, San Francisco, met and married a blond African boy from Rhodesia. In many ways, it seems like a fairy-tale love story, and I'm sure for those reading this, it might sound that way. "A blue-eyed boy meets a brown-eyed girl, oh-oh-oh, the sweetest thing."[15] After all, in 2021, they celebrated fifty years of marriage! And yet

---

[12] 2 Corinthians 11:30–31 (NIV).
[13] 2 Corinthians 10:17 (NIV).
[14] James 4:13–17 (NIV).
[15] U2, "Sweetest Thing," Track #8 on *The Best of U2 1980–1990*, Island Records, 1998, compact disc.

their story is really a story of God's faithfulness as they chose, and still choose to this day, to seek the Lord together. I could write another whole book about that story! In truth, the Lord has rewarded my parents for allowing the Holy Spirit to cultivate the soil of their hearts. It is also a testament to Granny and Grampa Maree that, to my knowledge, all of their children and spouses, grandchildren and their spouses, and even their great-grandchildren have made decisions to follow Christ.

It would seem only fitting with my *halo-halo* ancestral background that I would have a *halo-halo* name. *Tamarah* (Ta-ma-rah) is my first name. My father, a linguist, who has studied both Hebrew and Greek extensively, wanted each of his children to have a Hebrew name with biblical significance. Tamarah, with an *h*, is derived from the word *Tamar*, which is the Hebrew word for a "date palm tree."

As a child, I often wondered why my parents named me after a tree, a palm tree in particular. I discovered the palm tree has ties to the words *tall* and *graceful* and is also associated with the word *righteousness*. While I am far from righteous, a sinner by birth, Christ Jesus, because of His love for me, hung on a tree. He took my sin and, rising from the dead on the third day, clothed me in righteousness!

Psalm 92:12–13 states, *"But the godly will flourish like palm trees and grow strong like the cedars of Lebanon. For they are transplanted to the Lord's own house. They flourish in the courts of our God."* What a glorious picture of a healthy, thriving tree! Even King Solomon recognized the splendor of the palm tree as *"he decorated all the walls of the inner sanctuary and the main room* [of the temple] *with carvings of cherubim, palm trees and open flowers."*[16]

Around our home on the island of Babuyan stood tall coconut palm trees. These trees have strong, straight, tall trunks and can withstand heavy winds. They bend and sway but are hard to break. As a symbol of righteousness, the palm tree stands tall; its stature is straight and true. I realize now why my parents named me after the palm tree. I pray that my roots grow deep, my trunk tall and straight, and my branches (or fronds in the case of a palm tree) ever stretching up, reaching with all my might to my Savior. *"Even in old age they will still produce fruit; they will remain vital and green. They will declare, 'The Lord is just! He is my rock! There is no evil in him!'"*[17]

Mei Jin (May-Jin) is my Chinese name. It is also my middle name. *Mei* means beautiful, and *Jin* means precious. Basically, when you put my Hebrew name and my Chinese names together, I am a beautiful and precious palm tree. What more could a girl ask for! I eventually ended up trading in my French South African last name (Maree, from French/Huguenots origin) for an Irish one (O'Neal) by marrying my wonderful husband. Could I get any more mixed up?

While there is some humor in the meaning of my names, I am honored to have been given such lovely names. My parents thoughtfully named me, bestowing on me a blessing of righteousness, forever reminding me that I am beautiful and precious to them and in the sight of God. I am redeemed, forgiven, valuable, and loved. And so here, in Scripture, I am reminded of who I am

---

[16] 1 Kings 6:29 (NIV).
[17] Psalm 92:14–15 (NIV).

and who I am called to be. Tamarah: "*I am overwhelmed with joy in the LORD my God! For he has dressed me with the clothing of salvation and draped me in a robe of righteousness.*"[18] Mei Jin: "*Yet God has made everything beautiful for its own time. He has placed eternity in the human heart.*"[19] "*Do not be afraid, for I have ransomed you. I have called you by name; you are mine. For I am the LORD your God, the Holy One of Israel, your Savior. Others were given in exchange for you. I traded their lives for yours because you are* precious *to me. You are honored, and I love you*" (emphasis added).[20]

I believe names are important. There is great significance to the meaning of someone's name, and I believe that our names call us and challenge us to live our lives in a way that lives up to our names. I will be the first to tell you that I am full of sin and unrighteous in so many ways, and on many days, I feel anything but beautiful. But that doesn't change the name (or rather, names) my parents gave me, and it doesn't change the way that the Lord sees me. He knows all my names, and He calls me by each. He then gives me the tools and abilities I need to live up to my names. In reality, my names are but a shadow of His name. I am imperfect and unrighteous, but He is perfectly righteous. I am marred by sin, captured in this inadequate body. He is entirely and completely beautiful, without blemish. I am a mixture, a combination of parts. In essence, I am *halo-halo.* But my pieces, broken and misfit as they may be, fit together perfectly—a reflection of Christ's holiness and beauty.

---

[18] Isaiah 61:10 (NLT).
[19] Ecclesiastes 3:11 (NLT).
[20] Isaiah 43:1b, 3–4 (NLT).

As *halo-halo* as I may feel, the greatest truth is that Christ's broken body makes me whole. His death and sacrifice on the cross are complete and final. His resurrection forever grants me a place where all my misfit pieces will find their place. My "*halo-halo*ness" is my uniqueness. My uniqueness is God's creativity. God's creativity is His love for me. His love for me is my complete salvation.

Two

The Three Bs: "Bath, Potty, and Bed"

Through Christ Jesus the law of the Spirit who gives life has set you free from the law of sin and death.

Romans 8:2

My first bed was a dresser drawer. Yes, it was a shallow drawer from a dresser that was pulled out as far as it could go, lined with blankets, and made quite comfortable for me as a newborn infant. I'm sure many thoughts are running through your head as to why and how this was the case, so let me explain.

My parents were missionaries, serving with the Summer Institute of Linguistics (SIL) in the Philippines. They lived on the island of Luzon, the largest island in the northern Philippines, for most of the year in a small town called Bagabag. This was where the SIL Center was located. This center had its own facilities, such as a pool, elementary school, and library and was a place for families to live while they completed linguistic research and language translation. This is where I spent most of my childhood.

Every few months, however, our family would fly out to Babuyan, a remote island in the northernmost part of the Philippines. We would spend a month or two at a time as a family on Babuyan Island learning the language of the people there. My parents felt it was part of their calling in life to do linguistic research and eventually translate the New Testament into the language of the Ibatan people. The SIL Center, near the town of Bagabag, was a good seven to ten hours by car (depending on traffic and road conditions) from the capital city of Manila, and Babuyan was a one-and-a-half-hour flight in a small, single-prop, Helio Courier airplane from the town of Bagabag.

During the late 1970s and early 1980s, there were few medical facilities in the northern part of the Philippines that my parents felt were comfortable or safe places for delivering a baby. This was especially true since it was going to be a C-section delivery, which was how both my older sister and I came into the world. And so, when it was nearing the time of my due date, my parents made the long and uncomfortable trip by bus from Bagabag to Manila so that my mother could deliver me at the well-known Makati Medical Center in the business district of Manila.

While in Manila, they stayed at the SIL Guesthouse. I was told that their room was very small and may not have had enough space to fit a cot, or maybe there was no cot available for them to use, so they improvised by using the dresser drawer as my first bed. I, of course, have no recollection of sleeping in a dresser drawer. My older sister, who was just barely two at the time, had stayed at our home in Bagabag with Granny and Grandpa Maree (my father's parents), who had arrived from Canada for a special visit. They brought my sister to Manila shortly after I was born.

Our family traveled a lot during my growing-up years, and because of that, I have slept in many unique places and have considered many interesting objects good enough for a bed over the years. I suppose you can endure anything for a few nights! No matter what city or country we were in or what bed we slept in, however, my father would always tell us, "Don't forget the three *B*s!" before we went to bed. The three *B*s consisted of "bath, potty, and bed." You might be asking yourself the same question I asked my dad my entire childhood. "Dad, potty starts with a *p*, not a *b*!" to which my dad would always answer, "You're right!" The concept of the three *B*s will forever be a mystery; however, for my entire childhood, the "three *B*s" were always part of our bedtime routine.

I never really knew how vital consistency was until I had children of my own. Routines become quickly ingrained in family life once little ones arrive: feeding time, nap time, changing diapers time, brushing teeth time, "bath, potty, and bed" time, and waking up for school time. All these "times" may seem tedious when you are in the trenches at 2:00 a.m. feedings or at the end of a long day when you are trying to floss your toddler's teeth; however, they are important moments in the life of a child that lead to good, healthy habits later on in their adult life. Faithfulness to complete these daily tasks, to ensure that these "times" in the day do not go unchecked, is paramount to not only their survival as infants but also to their health and maturity as adults.

Now many years later, as I reflect on these practical daily routines, not only in my life but also in the lives of my children, I am reminded of God's goodness and faithfulness throughout my daily comings and goings. I have experienced the faithfulness of God in both the daily grind of work and school, and the significant moments that have defined my life. His faithfulness has followed me even when I have not honored Him by acknowledging His presence. His goodness has filled me even when I have filled my schedule to the brim and when my daily routine has not included time with Him. Second Timothy 2:13 says that "even if we are not faithful, he remains faithful. He must be true to himself" (NIV). He must be true to his character.

Because of God's faithfulness, I can say that my childhood was a good one. I truly have no complaints about the life I lived overseas, not only because it was "normal" to me but also because God's faithfulness and provision for my family overshadowed any difficulties or trying circumstances that we may have endured. It seemed very "normal" for our family to live in the Philippines. Other families that I knew lived in China or Germany, and still other families (particularly our own extended families) lived in far-off countries such as the United States of America or Canada.

Life was actually pretty grand for me during my elementary school years. Because we lived at the SIL Center, there were other international ex-patriot ("ex-pat") families who had children our age. We roamed the center barefoot after school, a small group of rowdy, sweaty-headed girls who climbed trees to reach tropical fruit. Our favorite fruit were guavas and mangoes that were hard, green, and sour as can be! My mouth is watering as I write this, and I can still taste the vinegary, peppery mixture all the missionary kids at the SIL Center affectionately referred to as "harry." If you made small teeth marks into the bite of sour, green mango or guava and dipped it into the "harry" concoction, the vinegar and soy sauce mixture would soak into the bite of fruit, giving it an even more tangy and delicious flavor. For some reason, only the kids seemed to enjoy this savory delicacy for an afternoon snack!

With all the tree climbing we did, it's a miracle that none of us were severely injured in our youth. Beyond a few broken limbs and an occasional stomachache from eating too many green guavas (or was it from drinking too much vinegar in the "harry" mixture?), our little troupe of girls managed to survive our elementary and middle school years without breaking our necks from falling out of trees. All jesting aside, I am convinced the Lord had angels specifically assigned to us to keep us safe as we jumped from limb to limb, stretching beyond the boundaries of safety to reach just one more mango. In fact, I believe He even delighted in our adventurous outdoor excursions. Despite our unruliness, I can imagine Him smiling at our inquisitiveness and resourcefulness, a small reflection of His grand creativity.

When we weren't on the hunt for the best mango trees to climb, our little group of friends would come up with all sorts of clever outdoor activities to pass the time until we were expected home for dinner. These undertakings ranged anywhere from making perfume out of hibiscus flowers to building a raft that we fully expected would hold our weight as we floated through the muddy pond in our backyard. We also loved to knock on the doors of various families who lived at the center to ask if we could "babysit" their infant children. I'm not sure why they ever agreed to let us take their children out for "babysitting," but somehow, they did, and we managed to return all said infants to their parents alive and well by the end of the day. They may have smelled like vinegar from their first taste of "harry," but in the end, the parents always seemed to say "yes" the next time we asked them if we could "babysit."

While my rambunctious group of friends and I appeared to be able to roam the place with very little supervision, we still had a set routine for our day. A typical day in our lives consisted of school, piano practice, homework, play or go swimming in the center pool, dinner, devotions, and finally bed. (Of course, we all would have rather placed the above-mentioned list in a different order or would have liked to have had more say in the allotment of time each item received, but nevertheless, this was roughly how our days played out.)

We were all aware of the "rules" that governed our little world. These rules brought consistency and shape to our days and at the same time a sense of freedom. We knew that if we stayed within the boundaries of these "rules," we were able to do as we pleased. One of these rules was to be home by dinner. School nights were different from weekend nights, of course, and as we got older, we were expected to help with dinner, but that gave us the freedom to play with our friends until that time. We also all knew which trees were "fair game" to climb and pick fruit from. These were the "center trees" that we did not need to ask permission to climb. Any trees that were on someone's property, however, required a knock on the door and a request for permission to climb and raid that particular tree of its fruit. Another rule was that if we went swimming, we logically had to have a parent present. The "wheeling and dealing" that went on to convince a parent to sit in the hot, tropical sun and "watch" us swim in an outdoor pool (which initially was not even covered) was a work of art. I'm sure our parents were all thrilled when we turned twelve so that we could follow a new set of rules and swim on our own as long as we had passed a swimming test and swam in a group of three.

There is an obvious parallel between the rules given to children for their safety and those that God gives us to guide us through our life as Christians. Living within the parameters of His love provides an immeasurable amount of freedom. The psalmist in Psalm 119 declares with joy and absolute conviction that his complete trust is in the promises given through the laws of God. Eternity for him hangs on the very Word of God. *"Never take your word of truth from my mouth, for I have put my hope in your laws. I will always obey your law, for ever and ever. I will walk about in freedom, for I have sought out your precepts."*[21]

Without restriction, we have limitless opportunities to come before the throne of God[22] to present our requests and divulge our fears and anxieties to a God Who sees every heartache and hears every declaration of sorrow, even if whispered from the very depths of our darkness. Christ's death and resurrection grant those who believe in Him freedom from the bondage of sin, which ultimately leads to death—a never-ending, eternal death. In place of death, we undeservingly receive freedom, hope, victory, and eternal life. *"Therefore, my friends, I want you to know that through Jesus the forgiveness of sins is*

---

[21] Psalm 119:43–45 (NLT).
[22] Ephesians 3:12.

proclaimed to you. Through him everyone who believes is set free from every sin."[23] What a gift to know that in Christ, we are free from condemnation and free from the fair punishment for our sins and even death itself!

As I said, my childhood was a good one, full of adventure and fun. I am thankful to my parents for accepting the call to start a new life in a new country and learn a new language, so that they might be an instrument, a tool, to share this profound freedom that they had themselves so deeply experienced through Christ. My growing-up years were merely a result of their obedience to God.

> The Spirit of the Sovereign Lord is on [them], because the Lord has anointed [them] to proclaim good news to the poor. He has sent [them] to bind up the brokenhearted, to proclaim freedom for the captives and release from darkness for the prisoners. [24]

And yet, how sad would it be if my parents were the only ones who received a calling from the Lord to preach the good news, to declare this gift of freedom? Because I can say that I have freedom in Christ, that Jesus is truly the Lord of my life, and that I am no longer held captive by sin, I can also say with conviction that "*the Spirit of the Sovereign Lord is on* me" and that He has sent *me* to "*pro-*

---

[23] Acts 13:38–39 (NLT).
[24] Isaiah 61:1 (NLT).

claim freedom for the captives." How much more personal and meaningful it is when I claim that passage for myself!

Perhaps this is one of the reasons I chose to write this book: to share with others what the Lord has done in my life. Jesus Christ rescued me from the slavery of sin and gave me, instead, a newness of hope that allows me to dream, to live with joy and purpose, and to look forward expectantly to the day when I will be able to see Jesus face-to-face. I don't live by a set of rules, but in the freedom that comes from knowing and loving Christ Jesus.

Tasha Layton released a song in 2022 called "Look What You've Done." The lyrics are powerful, and anytime I hear this song being played on the radio, I get goose bumps on my arms. If I'm driving to work and this song starts playing, I can't seem to stop myself as I belt out the words (with the windows rolled up, of course), singing from deep within my soul.

> On the cross, in the grave
> With a stone, rolled away
> All my debt, it was paid
> Look what You've done
>
> In my heart, in my mind
> In my soul, in my life
> With my hands lifted high
> I'm singing
> Look what You've done
>
> Look what You've done
> Look what You've done in me

> You spoke Your truth into the lies
> I let my heart believe
> Look at me now
> Look how You made me new
> The enemy did everything that he could do
> Oh, but look what You've done[25]

I have heard some say that being a Christian is limiting, restricting, and even boring. In my experience, being a Christ follower has been anything but dreary or tedious. The call to follow Christ, to be obedient to his Word, has certainly not been boring. I have reaped the benefits of my parents' decision to follow Christ but have, in time, learned to lean on the promises in God's Word and have experienced on my own the indescribable joy of knowing Christ.[26]

While routine, consistency, and even rules are factors that contribute to a meaningful and well-thought-out life, living a life in step with God's Word is paramount to experiencing the freedom that comes from truly knowing God. The apostle Paul states this so clearly in his letter to the Romans. "*Through Christ Jesus the law of the Spirit who gives life has set you free from the law of sin and death.*"[27] I love the way that Christian artist Big Daddy Weave reiterates this in his song "Redeemed." "*I am redeemed! You set me free! So I'll shake off these heavy chains, wipe away every stain. Now I'm not who I used to*

---

[25] Tasha Layton, "Look What You've Done," track #7 on *How Far*, BEC Recordings, 2022.
[26] 1 Peter 3:8b.
[27] Romans 8:2 (NLT).

be. I am redeemed! I'm redeemed!"[28] The very idea of heavy chains is wearisome and backbreaking, to say the least. Sin weighs on us until one day we are overtaken, and we succumb to death. Victory and freedom in Christ mean that *"Satan is suddenly silent. And you are suddenly jubilant. You realize that Satan cannot accuse you. No one can accuse you!"*[29] That is freedom! That is living!

Perhaps there is more to "the three *B*s" after all! My dad's way of helping us remember the rules for our bedtime routine somehow makes sense in my Christian life as well. When we align our lives with Christ's law of the Spirit, as it says in the book of Romans, we experience freedom from the "lies we let ourselves believe" and joy in knowing that our debt is paid and that we can face whatever challenges or difficulties might come our way.

Instead of simply following a routine of "bath, potty, and bed" to get us to the end goal of a good night's sleep, however, we can choose to align our hearts and our lives with something of much greater significance. I propose "believe, purpose, and boldness." Believe that Jesus is the Son of God Who died for our sins, paying the penalty that we never could. Believe that He rose again to conquer death, and because He was our voluntary, substitutionary atonement, we are therefore granted forgiveness of our sins and the gift of eternal life with Him.

Because we have been freed from the bondage of sin, we now have a purpose. We are deeply loved and cherished by God, so much so that He did not spare His own Son, Jesus, to die in our place. This should affect

---

[28] Bid Daddy Weave, "Redeemed," track #7 on *Love Come to Life*, Curb Records / Fervent Records, 2012.

[29] Max Lucado, *In the Grip of Grace: You Can't Fall Beyond His Love* (Nashville: W Publishing Group, 1996), 177.

how we live our lives. We have a new identity, and we have hope for the future and therefore live with purpose. Hebrews 10:23 encourages us to *"hold unswervingly to the hope we profess."*[30] And because we can live with purpose, we can also boldly and confidently approach God with our fears, worries, and doubts, knowing that He will answer, comfort, and sustain us.

The author of the book of Hebrews challenges us to *"approach the throne of grace with confidence, so that we may receive mercy and find grace to help us in our time of need."*[31] What a comfort that is! As I challenge myself, I also challenge you, my reader, to move beyond the simple adage of "bath, potty, and bed" and lean into "believe, purpose, and boldness." May you experience deep joy and comfort knowing that Jesus Christ has forever canceled your debt and, in the place of sin and death, has granted you newness of life! *"You were dead because of your sins and because your sinful nature was not yet cut away. Then God made you alive with Christ, for he forgave all our sins. He canceled the record of the charges against us and took it away by nailing it on the cross,"*[32] allowing us to live fully in the freedom of knowing Jesus Christ.

---

[30] Hebrews 10:23 (NIV).
[31] Hebrews 4:16 (NIV).
[32] Colossians 2:13–14 (NLT).

Three

Banana Prayers

*Call to me and I will answer you and tell you great
and unsearchable things you do not know.*

Jeremiah 33:3

"*Lord, if someone could just bring us a bunch of bananas today, that would be great!*" I can't remember how many times my mom prayed this prayer when we were kids. As missionaries, we lived on Babuyan, a remote island in the northern Philippines, for several months out of the year. Something as simple as a sweet banana could sound even more delicious than a bowl of ice cream after what seemed like endless weeks of eating only rice, squash, and beans. My mom's prayers for bananas always seemed to be miraculously answered, and she began to refer to them as her "banana prayers." She would remind us that God hears and answers all prayers (even if He doesn't answer right away), big prayers and small prayers, even prayers for bananas.

Prayer is powerful. I, too, believe that God hears every prayer, those shouted in the midst of life's storms and those uttered in silence from the depths of our being. I believe God heard every one of my mom's "banana prayers," and He answered them with real, tangible provisions.

The Philippines has many types of bananas, and Babuyan is no exception. It was a tropical paradise for fruit with all the rain and its rich volcanic soil, and the bananas were probably the sweetest, most delicious bananas I have ever eaten. The Ibatan have specific names for each type of banana that grows on the Island. My favorite type of banana was the *sa Manila* banana. Its name literally means "from Manila" because they were brought to Babuyan Island from Manila, the national capital located on the main island of Luzon. The *sa Manila* bananas are small, ladyfinger bananas with very thin skins and are as sweet as honey. They were so small you could almost eat one of these bananas in one bite. It was hard to stop eating them; they tasted so good.

As members of the Summer Institute of Linguistics (SIL), my parents were assigned to work among a small tribal group of people on a remote island off the northern coast of Luzon, Philippines. Every few months, our family would fly from the SIL Center in Bagabag, Nueva Vizcaya, where we lived in central Luzon, to Babuyan Island to stay about a month or two. We were there to learn the language and culture of the Ibatan people.

My linguist parents accomplished this by analyzing the language, producing literacy books, and working on the translation of the Scriptures into the Ibatan language. My sister and I accomplished this in quite a different, less academic way. We loved playing with the local schoolchildren and learning how to do various skills, such as carry firewood on our heads, pound rice without sloshing the rice still in its husks out of the hollowed-out tree trunk used for pounding rice, or how to identify the different types of local citrus trees, among other activities. All this, of course, took place when we weren't doing schoolwork or holding a flashlight for my dad while he did things like suture up a machete wound from an Ibatan who had been working in the fields.

The flight from the SIL Center to Babuyan took about one and a half hours one way, with about thirty minutes of the flight being over the open ocean on a small, single-prop, five-seater Helio Courier airplane. We were only allowed 750 pounds (and sometimes as few as 680 pounds!) for all our luggage and body weight. That worked just fine when my sister and I were babies, but as we grew, we soon found that the 750 pounds allotted to us was quickly consumed. So we packed the essentials—what was truly a necessity for our two-month stay: photocopied pages of school textbooks for me and my sister so we could complete our school assignments, our small battery-operated piano keyboard, my parents' Bible translation materials, instant coffee, medicine, flour, instant pudding mix, and cans of condensed milk and Vienna sausages. We were hopeful that the Ibatan would provide us with a few other fresh ingredients, such as fruit, vegetables, and, of course, rice—the Filipino staple. Sometimes we were given fish and, on rare occasions, chicken or pork, which we were very grateful for!

During certain seasons, our diet consisted largely of rice, squash, and beans. Basically, whatever the Ibatan people were generous enough to give us, we ate. This included anything from their fields during harvest season (rice, eggplant, peanuts, sugarcane, beans, squash, watermelon, pineapple, bananas, and lemons) and literally anything out of the ocean when the seas were calm enough to go spear fishing (octopus, squid, turtle, and any type of fish). The beautiful, colorful fish that you see swimming in tanks at aquariums are among many of the fish I have eaten, fresh out of the ocean. We found out that typically, the more vibrant the colors (like angelfish), the thicker the skin and the "fishier" and pastier it tasted. The less colorful the fish, the more delicious it was! It all sounds like a delightful tropical experience, but you must remember that we lived on an island with many areas of jungle, in a grass house with very little amenities, and certainly no chocolate bars or cookies in the early days. If an Ibatan happened to catch an octopus that day and was willing to share it with us, then we might end up having an octopus for dinner too! If the seas were too rough to fish, then we were stuck with rice, squash, beans, and perhaps a can of Vienna sausages. And so, the "banana prayers" began.

In many ways, the "banana prayers" were a reminder that God cared about the details of our lives. You might think that bananas are trivial, and indeed, in the grand scheme of things, they were. But in those days, a banana seemed like a real treat, and the Lord knew this. I suppose it might sound a little bit like the children of Israel complaining about something to eat in the desert. They grumbled to Moses about not having enough food to eat. And so, the Lord gave them *manna*, a nondescript wafer that became their lifeline—their "bread of life." He gave them just enough for what they needed that day. It was an exercise in faith, trusting that the Lord would continue to provide *manna* for them each day. Later, however, they complained about the *manna* and begged Moses to ask God for some meat. Out of the graciousness of His heart, He sent them quail. Again, just enough quail for the day.[33] In the same way, we trusted the Lord to provide our daily meals on Babuyan. Yes, I know, like the grumbling Israelites, I complained about the beans and squash, probably more than my parents wanted to hear and more than I care to admit. (And later, I probably complained about the bananas too!) But looking back, I see the banana prayers as an olive branch, daring to hope that there was something beyond the mundane, beyond the ordinary.

My mom believed that when she prayed, even for bananas, the Lord would hear and provide. *"'In those days when you pray, I will listen. If you look for me wholeheartedly, you will find me. I will be found by you', says the Lord."*[34] I realize this verse was written for the nation of Israel while they were in captivity, but let me tell you; there were times that I felt we might be in captivity to a land of rice and beans and squash! The point here is that the Lord hears us, takes note of our discomfort, and offers Himself up to be found by us. Sometimes, the Lord's provision for us was the octopus, but more often than not, He supplied us with a fresh bunch of sweet bananas, a way of showing His love and care for us. We don't have to pray in vain, hoping that someone will hear us. We pray with purpose and faith, knowing that we are praying to a God Who sees, hears, and takes delight in responding in a personal way.

There were numerous other opportunities for us to trust the Lord to provide for us. The flight to Babuyan was itself an exercise in faith. I remember thinking, *We*

---
[33] Exodus 16 (NIV).
[34] Jeremiah 29:12 (NIV).

are going to need more than banana prayers if we land in the ocean and get eaten by sharks, or if I die from excessive vomiting! (For the record, I don't recall having ever made it to Babuyan without throwing up at least once.) I dreaded the flight, the tiny, cramped space squeezed in between my mom and my sister, the loud noise of the engine, the smell of gasoline, and the incessant nausea.

Being the lightest, I was sometimes put in the very back seat with the rest of the cargo. Unlike everyone else, I had no access to a door, and every now and again, I joked that my family would forget about me in the back of the plane if we ever landed in the ocean. (There was an incident in Switzerland when I was six years old where my family left me behind on the third floor of a family friend's apartment after being told to go the bathroom before our road trip. I guess I took too long because, when I came out, everyone had gone down to the car! They didn't actually get in the car and leave, but we still joke about that time they "left" me by myself in Switzerland.)

There was a time, however, when we very nearly did land in the ocean. I was about ten or eleven when I thought we might have to use the water crash testing procedures we had practiced at the community swimming pool at the SIL Bagabag Center. The winds thrashed the little plane up and down, sideways and every which way imaginable, and the turbulence felt like a violent roller-coaster ride. I thought we would hit the ocean waves beneath us. When the plane banked, I remember my mother saying she could count the fish in the ocean. I, on the other hand, was far from worried about how many fish were beneath us. I had already lost my breakfast, snack, drink, and whatever remained of my stomach contents, and even my stomach lining, at that point.

For some reason, my mom, sister, and I were sitting three across in the middle of the plane for this trip. We must have had a lot of luggage, as the back of the plane was full. The turbulence was so bad that even my mom and sister had been throwing up. We had run out of plastic bags, and at that point, the three of us were literally sharing the last bag! Talk about family bonding! Our plane had one tiny square window (just an air vent) measuring about two inches by two inches. It had an even tinier screw you could barely twist with your fingers to open up about a quarter of an inch. My face was plastered to this opening, trying to catch a whiff of fresh air and praying with all my might that it would all just be over. I couldn't tell which was worse, my fear of crashing into the ocean or the desperation I felt that my nausea would never end.

Another time, we did have a crash landing, miraculously not in the ocean but on land. The culprit, of course, was the strong wind that pushed the little plane down as we approached the island and made our final descent to land. As we hit the ground, the landing gear snapped, whipping the plane around ninety degrees and sending it speeding into the nearby bushes that lined the landing strip, branches flying across the windshield.

We were all relatively unharmed, aside from the gash on my dad's forehead, a few bumps and bruises, and sore necks and backs the next day from the impact. The Lord certainly protected us from far greater injuries and allowed the plane to be fixed on site (and after another plane arrived, bringing extra parts). It took a couple of weeks before enough repairs were completed so that it could be flown off the island. (The repairs included wing repair, a new landing gear, engine and engine mount replacement, rudder repair, and a new prop.)

The pilots who flew our family out to Babuyan were the incredible, highly skilled JAARS (Jungle Aviation And Radio Service) pilots. I know we could never repay them for taking their lives into their hands each time they flew us out to Babuyan. JAARS pilots work in close connection with Bible Translation teams to help them gain quicker access (and in some cases, the only access available) to remote locations around the world. JAARS pilots have extensive training to fly planes, such as the Helio Courier that can take off and land in incredibly short distances. Ultimately, however, the fact that we are all still alive after the countless flights, takeoffs, and landings is miraculous, and praise for our safety truly belongs to the Lord. His protection over my family and the pilots who flew us out to Babuyan time and time again is nothing short of a miracle.

I often wondered, jokingly, if the pilots ever drew straws to see who would have to fly my family to and from Babuyan. Perhaps it was because, when flying to Babuyan, we often encountered strong winds, or maybe it was because it required them to land on the (mostly level) grass airstrip that my dad and other Ibatan had made by hand with machetes and other handmade farm tools.

My dad worked on making three different airstrips on that Island. The first one was at the top of a steep hill. We all hated walking up the jungle path in our flip-flops for almost thirty minutes to get to the airstrip, especially when it had recently rained. The Ibatan thought little of the trek, even as they carried our cardboard boxes of supplies on their shoulders. They did this all the time. Most of them lived on the sides of mountains. On either side of the upper airstrip was farmland cut out of the dense jungle. The second airstrip was built at a lower elevation, but the pilot didn't think this airstrip was in a good location, so a third airstrip was eventually built. This one was built at sea level to combat the fierce winds that would often whip over the mountaintop airstrip. However, because it was at sea level (just a few hundred yards from the shoreline), there was literally only a fence separating the grass airstrip from the humongous boulders along the shore that formed the "beach."

I can remember a time when we were scheduled to fly out to Babuyan. My mom began praying because terrible weather was predicted. "Lord," she prayed, "if You want us to go to Babuyan tomorrow, please make it clear. If it rains tomorrow, we will know we aren't supposed to go." The Lord heard her "banana prayer," although we all asked her to be a little more specific when we woke up at five in the morning and it was drizzling, a light sprinkle. The rain was barely making the grass wet! *Is this considered rain?* we all wondered.

After calling the pilot to determine his opinion, the decision was made to "try." To "try" meant that we would execute the mission as planned, knowing there was a high probability that we might have to abort said mission. If we turned around, that would also mean up to three hours of turbulent flying. (I can remember one time during bad weather and heavy cloud cover the pilot was unable to find the island. We flew five minutes in every direction, then ten minutes. At some point, we turned back so we wouldn't run out of gas.) "Better add some more plastic bags for Tami," someone said, "and make sure to use the bathroom." I groaned audibly, "Why are we doing this again?" I was already sick to my stomach from having been up so early, not eating much for breakfast for fear that I would just throw it up on the flight.

Waiting in the hangar and smelling the fumes as they fueled up the plane didn't seem to help my situation. We all weighed in to make sure that we had an accurate weight total for the plane, especially if we would be encountering bad weather; we didn't want the plane to be over the allotted weight limit.

After loading the cargo, we crammed into the airplane (I was sitting in the very back) and taxied out and took off. It was still drizzling. None of us, not even the pilot, would dare to call it "rain" for fear that we would be turning a blind eye to the obvious answer that the Lord had given us. Eventually, we reached a point where the pilot decided to turn back. My dad and I were sick, and I had collected a few bags of throw-up. My mom and sister had also lost their breakfast.

The pilot decided visibility was too poor and the winds were too strong to land on the island. We could almost see Babuyan. But it would be too dangerous to try and land, and we were getting low on fuel, so the pilot turned the plane around. Another hour of nausea followed. When we finally landed safely back in the hanger, we all agreed on two things: next time, my mom would be more specific with her prayers and that "sprinkling" or even "drizzling" counted as rain!

My mom's banana prayers didn't always turn out as we had hoped (as in the "sprinkling rain"), and because of that, I often questioned the validity of those prayers. Did that person just happen to walk up to our house with a bunch of bananas he didn't want? Didn't they just give us those eggplants because they were tired of eating them themselves? What I began to discover, however, was that while the "prayers of the righteous are powerful and effective," unless those prayers were *my* prayers, I wasn't truly able to celebrate the answers to those prayers.[35]

I began to wonder what would happen if I, too, prayed. Of course, there were always things that we prayed for as a family, and that I even prayed for on my own, but what could I truly pray for with a prayer that came right from my heart? Would God really hear my prayers, and would He answer them? I found myself really praying when we had family devotions, not just listening to my parents pray, but earnestly seeking God along with them. Because I began to join in praying, asking God for answers, I began to share in the victory and the blessings of answered prayers.

Every four to five years, missionaries with Wycliffe Bible Translators and the Summer Institute of Linguistics left the mission field that they were assigned to (in our case, the Philippines) to spend one year in their home country. The purpose of this year was to reconnect with friends and family and become reacquainted with the culture of their home country.

During my eighth-grade year, my family left the Philippines for one such scheduled furlough. My parents felt it was important to establish a home base somewhere in North America instead of living in a new area each time we left the Philippines for a furlough. The Summer Institute of Linguistics had launched a new training school on the campus of Trinity Western University in Canada as part of both their undergraduate and graduate linguistics programs and had asked my dad to teach lin-

---
[35] James 5:16 (NIV).

guistics there. Because some of my dad's family was living close by in that area, my parents felt that Langley, British Columbia, would be a perfect location.

They enrolled both me and my sister in a public school, the Fort Langley Fine Arts School in the neighboring town of Fort Langley. You can imagine that I might have needed a few prayers to help me navigate my first year of high school in a public school. I prayed every day that God would give me a friend. And He did.

There was one sweet girl in eighth grade that became an instant friend. I'm not exactly sure what she saw in me. I was quirky, wore the wrong clothes, said the wrong things, was clueless about anything popular, had no idea how to talk to boys, and certainly had never had a locker or changed classes before. This dear friend was a dance major, and I was a music major, so our classes rarely intersected, but we did have a few periods together. We made sure to always sit together whenever we could, have lunch together, and even try to get on the same team for PE if possible. Neither of us were very good at sports. I certainly had no clue how to play hockey. Since it seemed like every Canadian I had met so far knew how to play hockey, I was surprised that she was just as clueless as I was.

I remember that she was disappointed when I broke my finger and was allowed to go to the weight room for the duration of the PE hockey season. Without any such ailments herself, my friend was forced to continue to play hockey with the rest of the PE class without me. Other than that, we were always together. Although we drifted apart after I moved back to the Philippines, and I haven't seen or spoken to this dear eighth-grade friend in many years, I honestly believe that she was a direct answer to prayer. Thank you for being my friend!

The time, however, that I truly knew that God had answered a desperate plea of mine was a few months after school had started during that same eighth-grade year. As a music major at the Fort Langley Fine Arts School, I was required to participate in various small-group ensembles. These ensembles performed at a certain number of public spaces each semester. Our woodwind ensemble was chosen to play a few pieces at both the Fort Langley Community Hall and the Fort itself in Fort Langley. The Fort is a national historic site, open for tours and recreated to look like it did in the 1800s. The Fort was a place where the Hudson's Bay Company, California gold prospectors, and First Nations interpreters had lived and mingled together. In the cold, our fingers were freezing. After managing to squeak out the minimum requirement of songs, we packed up and hightailed it out of there. It wasn't until I got home that I realized I had left my flute somewhere inside the Fort.

Living in a third-world country for most of my early life taught me that you never, ever left anything unattended. It was as good as gone if you turned your head, or especially if you left it out in the open as I had done with my flute. I just knew it was stolen. I also knew that my parents could not afford to buy me a new flute. The one I had was purchased at a pawnshop in San Francisco while visiting my grandparents, and there was no way we would be able to go back there to buy a new one. That was my first problem. My second problem was that I was terrified of talking on the phone. The only phone we had in our home at the SIL Center in the Philippines was an old rotary phone that was only hooked up for internal calls to other missionaries. I rarely ever spoke on the phone, and if I did, it was to answer it and hand it to my parents. I hardly ever spoke on the phone to my friends because we played together every day after school. I never spoke on the phone to strangers. With the slightest possibility that my flute was picked up by a staff member and held in the lost-and-found bin at the Fort, someone had to call and find out.

Since I was the one who had forgotten my flute, I had to make the call. I had no idea who to ask and was terrified that the person on the other end would scold me for leaving my flute behind. What was even worse was that I had been dropped off at home by a friend, and my parents were not yet home. I had to at least find out if my flute was still at the Fort before my parents came home.

This seemed like an impossible situation to me. My twelve-year-old mind was completely convinced that, by this time, my flute was in the hands of a total stranger, a random person who didn't even play the flute or like music but was instead going to sell my precious flute to the highest bidder.

I prayed fervently, tears streaming down my face, for the courage to pick up the phone and dial the number. *Lord, if You could please have someone nice answer the phone and not scold me, and more importantly, please let them have my flute!* Of course, no one yelled at me when I called. The person on the other end of the phone was, to my great surprise and relief, quite nice and sympathetic. Better yet, they had my flute! How ridiculous, you might think. I, on the other hand, was convinced this was a miracle that only the Lord could have done and fell to my knees, sobbing and thanking the Lord that he had allowed me to find my flute! I learned that day that

God did hear my prayers and, more importantly, cared enough about my dire situation to answer them! I knew then, by personal experience, the power of prayer and the kindness of the Lord to answer.

Philippians 4:6 says that we are not to be anxious about *anything*. That certainly would look like peace if we were free from anxiousness. I had been beside myself with worry about my lost flute. Looking back on that situation, I had probably worked up the circumstances in my head so much that it was a bigger ordeal for me than it needed to be. The point is, however, that it doesn't matter how big of a deal the situation might be to you or to someone else, we can still pray about it.

The apostle Paul goes on to say that, in fact, *"in every situation, by prayer and petition, with thanksgiving,"* we are to *"present our requests to God."* Every situation, not just some situations that others deem important. If they are important to you, then you should pray, even if you are simply praying for a bunch of sweet bananas! The best part is this: *"And the peace of God which transcends all understanding, will guard your heart and your mind in Christ Jesus."*[36] Who doesn't want peace that transcends all understanding? This peace can only be found in the perfect love of Christ Jesus.

Richard J. Foster states that *"trust is confidence in the character of God."* We know that God is faithful, that He keeps His word, and that His plans are for our good.[37] If that is true, then we can believe that God is trustworthy. If God is in control and if we can trust Him, then we can trust His character. Imagine if we could then truly *"give it*

---

[36] Philippians 4:6–7 (NIV).
[37] Jeremiah 29:11 (NIV).

all into his hands and then turn around and walk away."[38] Could we truly walk away in confidence and complete surrender, knowing that He is in complete control, even if the outcome of our prayer is not what we had originally asked for?

---

[38] Richard J. Foster, *Prayer*, 24, 56.

Four

Stage Fright

And we boast in the hope of the glory of God.

Romans 5:2b

I have always been shy and lacking in self-confidence. As a child, I was envious of all the "outgoing kids" who seemed to have no trouble getting up onstage, auditioning for a speaking or singing part in a play, or even raising their hand in class to answer a question.

For me, even though I was shy, having to sit in the front row in class was both necessary and mortifying. It was necessary because my eyesight was terrible. I couldn't quite see what my teacher had written on the chalkboard, even in fourth grade when I finally got glasses (yes, an actual blackboard that the teacher wrote on with white chalk). Mortifying because sitting in the front row placed me in the direct line of sight of my teacher and in full view of all my classmates.

Seeing clearly has always been difficult, and while I am very thankful to my parents for getting me glasses when I needed them, that was another significant blow to my self-confidence. Back in the '80s, big pink, plastic glasses went marvelously with the frizzy, aqua-net bangs that we all insisted on wearing. My eyesight eventually became so poor that my glasses did actually look like the bottom of a coke bottle.

Looking back at my pictures from elementary and middle school, I am thankful I didn't also have metal braces to complete the look (those came later in life, in my thirties). I'm now in my forties, and I'm still practically blind without my glasses. And so, I am very thankful to the Lord that He gave someone a brilliant mind to invent contacts since that revolutionized my high school experience!

While glasses did help me see well enough to be able to read what was on the chalkboard at school, they certainly did nothing to help me in the sports department, where depth perception was still a real problem. We were always dripping with sweat anyway since the Philippines had a constant temperature of about 90 degrees and 95 percent humidity. The combination of a perpetually sweaty face and an Asian nose meant that my glasses never had a chance of staying on my face. This, of course, made it hard to run, bike, or climb trees, and worst of all, it was nearly impossible to play "capture the flag" on Friday nights with the rest of the missionary kids at the SIL Center. I was always running into things.

One Friday night, playing "capture the flag" in the darkness, I got the wind knocked right out of me when I ran full force into a wire clothesline. The house owners were supposed to tie a white cloth on the clotheslines on Friday nights to avoid such things as this, but for some reason, they had forgotten, and I ran right into it. It was the perfect height for my neck, and when I hit it, it flung me backward. I landed hard flat on my back, knocking the wind (and any chances of me capturing the flag) right out of me. For a week after that incident, it hurt to swallow, and I had to explain to everyone why I had a red line across my neck.

Running into the clothesline was not an isolated incident. I can't tell you how many sliding glass doors I have walked into throughout my life. As a kid, it was difficult to find out which of the large glass doors to the entrance of the mall, or even a store, were open and which were shut. Even with glasses, my depth perception was off, and I would plow right into the glass wall. I learned to look for the door handles to determine whether a door was open or shut instead of trying to make out whether or not there was a glare on the glass. Perhaps that's why I was prone to so many headaches in elementary and middle school!

If wearing glasses wasn't enough, I spent quite a few months out of the year on crutches during middle school. I was growing so fast that my body couldn't quite keep up with my height. Skinny, lanky, and awkward, I was certainly not coordinated. In fact, my childhood nickname, lovingly bestowed on me by my elementary school friends was "*chicken ninny,*" revealing just how awkward I actually was. While I could climb trees barefoot better than any of the boys at the SIL Center, the combination of being half-blind and having sore joints meant that I was terrible in sports, and even worse when it came to catching things.

Baseball was perhaps the session of PE that I dreaded the most. I couldn't ever quite see the ball clearly enough to hit it when the pitcher threw it at me. I was convinced he was purposely throwing it at my head. Either that or he had terrible aim. Both scenarios were entirely possible during a fifth-grade PE class. Even if I could miraculously see the ball in time, squinting into the blazing sun, I couldn't coordinate my arms to swing the bat in time. I was so afraid the ball would hit my glasses and then I wouldn't be able to see anything. When the nightmare of being up to bat was over, the dreaded outfield awaited. If I couldn't see the ball when it was being pitched to me, how on earth was I supposed to see a white ball fifty feet above me against a background of white clouds? If I ever caught a ball, it was a miracle. If I ran after it and stepped wrong, I ended up with a sprained ankle or a torn ligament. I couldn't ever decide whether crutches were actually a fair trade or not for not having to play baseball.

Not being able to see well made me awkward and certainly affected my lack of confidence. I suppose I never really grew out of the shyness; I just became more adept at hiding it. I was determined, however, to not let this deter me from being involved in school activities. I purposely put myself in challenging situations to help me learn to overcome my shyness. It's possible that's why I auditioned for an acting part for my high school senior play. The ironic thing was that I was cast as Lily Belle from John Patrick's *The Curious Savage*. Lily Belle was a most undesirable, arrogant, loudmouthed, self-assured, spoiled, and insulting character who had been married five times and had her sneaky eye on an even bigger jackpot.

Standing onstage with several layers of blue eye shadow completing my sultry look, I cleverly hid my feelings of being completely mortified under the rookie guise of a first-time actor's stage fright. My self-confidence didn't get any better by playing the obnoxious character Lily Belle, as you might have guessed. I continued to doubt myself in almost everything I did, analyzing the minutia of what I could have done better and subjecting myself to what I felt to be a total embarrassment when I made mistakes that I knew others could possibly criticize me for.

The grand stage was never my ideal "comfort zone," but I began to find solace in playing the piano. I fell in love with the piano when I started taking lessons at the age of four. My first keyboard was a tiny, battery-operated Casio that had miniature-sized keys with barely three octaves. We were able to take it with us on our flights to Babuyan because it was so light, not adding much to the weight allowance on the plane. This was a way for me and my sister to continue practicing while on a remote island with my parents. Even as a young child of five or six, I realized that I had quickly outgrown what to me was a toy piano, so I drew "extensions" for the keyboard on pieces of cardboard, imagining the sound the hand-drawn keys would make as I played them. Realizing this, my parents upgraded the miniature Casio to a keyboard that at least had full-size keys, even if it didn't have all seven octaves. Eventually, they purchased a "real" acoustic piano for our home at the SIL Center in Bagabag from another missionary family so that I could practice on full-size keys and use the pedals. I knew this must have been a financial sacrifice for my parents, and I am grateful that I was able to practice on a "real" piano during my elementary and middle school years.

By the time I reached high school (an international boarding school called Faith Academy, located in the capital city of Manila, about eight to ten hours from the SIL Bagabag Center), I had performed in numerous terrifying recitals. At the age of eleven, I had also been placed on the rotation as a church pianist for Sunday evening and oftentimes Sunday morning worship services at the SIL Center in Bagabag. I had even played for a few weddings. All of these experiences were excellent preparation for high school when I was provided with the opportunity to be the pianist for the high school senior concert and jazz choirs during both my eighth and ninth-grade years. For some reason, it never really bothered me to play the piano in front of an audience as long as I was accompanying others and not being featured as the soloist.

During my last year of high school, I was given the honor of opening the senior piano recital with all three movements of Mozart's "Piano Sonata in F Major." I knew it inside and out, had meticulously marked up and analyzed my score, and had sacrificed hours of my free time practicing and committing it all to memory. However, as I sat down at the piano in the middle of the stage, I knew I was doomed. I looked blankly at the black-and-white keys in front of me and realized I couldn't find my starting notes. I couldn't even find middle C! *Where has it gone? How am I supposed to play thirteen pages of music from memory when I can't even find middle C?* I decided to start my piece anyway, hoping that as I played, my fingers would remember what they were supposed to do.

Any musician will tell you, however, that you can't simply rely on rote memory or finger muscle memory to perform that many pages of music from memory. An inexperienced performer at the age of sixteen, I was naive. After only just a few bars, I was in trouble, and I knew it. Before I could change my mind, I did the unthinkable. I simply stopped playing and walked offstage. Fortunately, I had the presence of mind to grab my music from backstage. I then proceeded to march back out to the piano onstage and restart my song. I ended up playing the entire sonata with my music in front of me, without ever even turning a page. I imagined that my parents, seated in the front row, were horrified. Of course, they weren't, but I'm sure they were holding their breath to see if I would make it through the song without walking offstage again!

My shyness at times prevented me from fully experiencing freedom from worry. Although my timid nature didn't stop me from trying difficult things, I was often so worried about what other people thought of me that it made me doubt if I could even accomplish what I had spent hours and even years working toward. I know I am not alone with these feelings and that many others have experienced similar situations, but I have, on many occasions, been deeply frustrated with myself because my nerves got the better of me when I failed to perform a difficult piece of music the way I could during my practices.

Even when I did do well, I would be so worried about what others thought that I wasn't fully able to celebrate my achievements. *What if they didn't think I was as good as I thought I was? What if they didn't like how I played? What if they noticed a mistake?* The proverbial *they* was always the most critical judge of any type of accomplishment I had. Even as I write this book, I wonder, *Will anyone ever read this? What if they don't like it? What if they don't understand it? What if they don't even finish it? What if? What if?*

In addition to my musical endeavors, I decided to try out for the volleyball team during my freshman year of high school. Perhaps this was partly because I loved being active but mostly because I wanted to prove that I could actually play a sport. (Although by this time I was wearing contacts and had finally stopped growing at such a rapid pace, I chose volleyball over tennis or softball because the size of the ball was bigger!) Amazingly, I made the team and ended up playing volleyball all four years in high school. The sad thing is, I was sometimes so worried about the fans in the stands watching me that it often affected my performance. Each time I rotated to the serving position, I knew all eyes would be on me, and I would pray that the ball would make it over the net. If it didn't, I felt defeated and devastated inside because I just knew my teammates, my coaches, the fans, and even the other team, were probably disappointed in me. I was often so stressed about serving that I failed to truly enjoy the rest of the game.

After graduating from high school at Faith Academy in the Philippines, I somewhat reluctantly moved to Canada with my parents. My sister, who had graduated from high school the year before, had already moved to Canada to start school at Trinity Western University in Langley, British Columbia. This left me and my parents behind in the Philippines so that I could finish my senior year and graduate with my class. I say I left reluctantly because, while the possibility of a new adventure as I started university was a thrilling concept, I was truly leaving all that I knew and had come to love behind: my friends, my home, my way of life, and my culture. In essence, I was saying goodbye to my childhood, taking with me only pictures and memories, to begin a new life in a place that was unfamiliar and unknown. I knew deep down, however, that I couldn't stay in the Philippines, trapped in childhood. I had to move on to the next adventure that was waiting for me.

All my friends were in the same boat, leaving the Philippines for college or university in a foreign land, the land their parents called "home." For me and many of my "missionary kid" friends, we were not only leaving behind our home, but we were also leaving the place of our birth, a place we had come to know as our *sariling bayan*, our homeland. Ironically, even today, when I come to the part of the Canadian national anthem that says, "My home and native land," I feel somewhat like an impostor singing those words.

While I have never doubted my patriotism to either the United States or Canada, many times I have felt as though I were living in between worlds, "standing on guard" for Canada, while at the same time holding my hand over my heart to sing about the "land of the free" and simultaneously declaring the "blaze of my heart" for "the Pearl of the Orient." What could I do to rectify the turmoil in my heart at leaving the land of my birth with the lands of my citizenship where my loyalties lay?

Change is hard. Moving is hard. The disruption generated by the physical move created an inner mayhem, a commotion of feelings with roots of sorrow deeply embedded in my heart. I knew in my head that, with time, pain would eventually turn into memories, but my heart refused to be comforted for quite some time after I left the Philippines. I was confident that one day the wounds from separation and what seemed like an upheaval in my life would heal and I would begin to create new memories, but in the interim, I felt as though I was in mourning.

I started college at Trinity Western University at the age of seventeen, caught between childhood and adulthood, wedged into a corner where I was forced to choose the grown-up world. I had never had a bank account before and had certainly never had my own checkbook. I also needed to pass a driving test so that I could drive myself to classes. I had decided not to live on campus as my parents would be living in Canada that year, just fifteen minutes from the university, so getting my driver's license (and a car) was imperative. While I had taken driver's ed in high school, my parents insisted on signing me up for driving school (which I am now thankful for). Miraculously, I passed my driving test and got my license, but once again I felt like an impostor. I would have to fake my way into adulthood by looking the part.

There was another hurdle to overcome, however, on my fast-tracked journey to adulthood. I needed a job. How on earth was I supposed to go about accomplishing that? I had absolutely nothing to put on a résumé (and what was a résumé anyway?). The only job I ever had that had actually generated any income was babysitting or playing the piano for an occasional wedding. I managed to land a temporary job in the mailroom at the university, sorting mail and stuffing envelopes, but after a few weeks when the job was complete, I was again left wondering how on earth I was supposed to get a job.

CanIL eventually offered me a job as their receptionist, which I gladly accepted. The CanIL office (Canada Institute of Linguistics) is SIL's linguistics training school in Canada. It is also the linguistics department of Trinity Western University, where my dad taught linguistics during that furlough year and were my mom worked in the finance office. I am still grateful to CanIL to this day for the experience of working in their office. I not only learned the necessary skills for holding down a job, but I also gained valuable insight into the rigorous requirements of becoming a Bible translator.

Although Trinity Western was a relatively small university, I had come from an even smaller high school where I knew every student and faculty member and lived in a dorm full of girls who became as close as sisters. I was now attending a university on a campus where the only person I knew was my sister. It seemed as though the progress I had made in high school to push past my introverted boundaries had all been for nothing. I drove to school praying for a friend, but instead, I walked from class to class in solitude, longing for friendship and companionship while at the same time praying that I would be able to get through the day without having to interact with too many people. I threw myself into my studies, taking up to twenty semester hours in one semester while working as many hours as I could at the linguistics office.

During my senior year of college, I decided to simultaneously work toward a piano performer's degree while finishing my undergraduate degree in English literature. I had previously been working toward a double major in English literature and secondary education, but I decided in my junior year that classroom instruction was not my thing. While I was driven and focused, working my way through college so that I could graduate debt-free, I was now nineteen years old but looked closer to fifteen. The twelve- and thirteen-year-olds in my seventh and eighth-grade split class that I student taught twice a week could sense my youth and my insecurity. I knew this when I showed up to class on my first day and they asked me if I was a new student. *Could they not see my visitor's name badge?* I thought. I panicked, and instead of stepping up to help the teacher teach, I was relegated to decorating the bulletin board. I ended up dropping the education major portion of my college career and picked up a minor in Christianity and Culture instead, hoping that I would learn something profound about the North American Christian culture and where I fit in. I still wanted to teach but couldn't imagine myself at that age having my own classroom full of kids who looked like they were nearly the same age as me (or at least so I thought).

To prove to myself (and possibly others) that I not only had the chops to play Rachmaninoff and Liszt or Barber and Bach's Partitas but that I could also play on a stage under someone else's scrutiny, I decided to also pursue the ARCT degree in piano performance with the Royal Conservatory of Music (RCM). Although based in Toronto, Canada, I was able to study with private teachers and take my exams, along with other hopeful ARCT students, at local exam centers in the Vancouver area. My prayer, however, was that I would never have to actually perform. I also began teaching piano to young beginners and found that I still enjoyed teaching, as long as it wasn't in a classroom with students the same size as me!

My pursuit of a performer's degree did end up requiring me to do some performing later on. The size of my studio began to grow, and with over fifty students performing at my recitals, that meant there were at least two hundred people in attendance. Accompanying my vocal students, playing duets with my piano students, and opening the recitals with solo pieces placed me more on the stage than in my seat. I also realized very quickly that no one else was going to walk up the stairs to the microphone onstage and welcome the parents, grandparents, and the multitude of other guests my eager students had invited to hear them play. I was the teacher, and I had to do it. My sweaty palms and trembling hands were almost imperceptible as I would hold the mic, smiling while giving my opening remarks. Inside, however, I was a quivering mess. After giving my welcome and any announcements parents needed to hear, I would make my way to the grand piano on the stage and play the opening piece. I knew I would have to subject my fingers, ice-cold from nervousness, to play whatever notes I commanded them to.

In the end, I was really the only one who ever knew if I skipped a section, repeated a section, or ended the song early because I couldn't bear to be subjected to the audience's scrutiny anymore. Somehow, I always finished and bowed gracefully no matter how I felt, but I'm sure none of the parents in the audience ever realized how quickly I wanted off that stage! This nervousness never went away. So much so that, fifteen years after I began teaching, and after a particular performance, I literally slid down the stairs, stilettos, pencil skirt, and all! Talk about mortification! This was the epitome of disaster! Fortunately, only half the audience who was seated on the side of the stairs where I had gracefully landed saw what really happened. I guess the other half of the audience left the recital wondering why one of my students shouted out, *"Are you okay, Ms. Tami?"*

I have learned over the years that my worry and fear of what the audience might think do very little to help me play better or speak with more confidence or authority. Remembering the joy of music and why I love to play the piano in the first place is a much better approach to handling my nerves, that and a lot of prayer. Minutes before any recital, you will find me in a bathroom stall, rehearsing what I will say to the parents and then praying fervently that God would help me make it through the opening remarks and get through my piano solo without a hang-up. I still go through this process after nearly twenty-five years of teaching and performing at student recitals.

What I have discovered is that my extreme nervousness and fear put me in a place of complete dependence on God. When I have practiced and rehearsed to the best of my abilities, all that I have left in my arsenal is to pray and ask the Lord for some serious help. In reality, how many parents really remember the few notes I missed? Hopefully no one! (They might remember me falling down the stairs, however!) But more importantly, I pray they will remember my attitude, my demeanor, how I greeted them, and the way I treated their children.

Standing in the bathroom stall before a recital, I still pray for a good performance, but I also pray that I would shine with grace and with the joy that the Lord has given me, that I would display the passion I have for music, and that I would truly depict to others the gift that music really is. Johann Sebastian Bach is credited for saying that *"the aim and end of all music should be none other than the glory of God and the refreshment of the soul."* If the way I play the piano at a recital reveals even a small glimmer of God's creativity and leaves the audience with a measure of contentment, then I have completed the task the Lord has set before me.

Some performances certainly go smoother than others, but when I choose to recognize that my worth as a teacher, a musician, or a performer does not come from the audience's perception of how well my recital went or how accurately I performed my solo, I am far less nervous. My worth comes from the fact that I am a child of God. I am created in His image, forgiven of my sins through the death of His Son on the cross, redeemed by His grace, and granted life eternal by the power of His resurrection. When you consider this, what else could be more important? My shyness and the insecurities I feel because of what other people might think of me or my feelings of not belonging should pale in comparison to the concern I should feel about what my Father in heaven thinks about how I treat others and how I handle others' disappointment in me.

I recently read a book by Allie Beth Stuckey titled *You're Not Enough (And That's Okay): Escaping the Toxic Culture of Self-Love*. I believe she accurately describes a pervasive way of errant thinking in our culture today. What we deem as "self-love" is actually selfishness. We are so worried about what others think of us that we spend an inordinate amount of time making sure that we take care of our public image and spend a shockingly little amount of effort on our inward image that is actually more important. Stuckey states,

> Because of Jesus, we have an answer to our insecurities, our self-criticism and self-doubt, and it's so much better than flimsy, shallow self-love. Our answer is him, the eternal, unchanging Creator and Sustainer of the universe, who paid for our sins on the cross, declaring us forever forgiven, innocent and righteous before a just and holy God.

Amen! What more, truly, could we ask for in life? And yet we continually allow ourselves to get so wrapped up in ourselves—our interests, our dreams, what we deserve—focusing on what will "fix" us that we forget we are, as Stuckey says, "*less than 'not enough'; on our own, we're nothing.*" Christ's sacrifice on the cross was final and perfect. We therefore have all the confidence we need knowing that we are "irrevocably purchased," redeemed, and made whole.[39]

Alisa Childers reiterates this concept in the book *Mama Bear Apologetics*, which she coauthored. In the chapter titled "I'm Not Religious; I'm Spiritual," Childers refutes society's claim that "*you are enough*" by stating that Scripture reveals the opposite. "*You are absolutely, most definitely* not *enough. You are so desperately not enough that it would be impossible to even calculate your not-enoughness.*" She goes on to say that "*this is actually good news! In fact, it's the whole point of Christianity: We are all sinners in desperate need of a Savior.*"[40]

Scripture is clear on this issue as well. The apostle Paul writes to the Ephesians, telling them and reminding us that "*it is by grace we have been saved.*" I love the way the New Living Translation translates this verse because it is so clear: "*God saved you by his grace when you believed. And you can't take credit for this; it is a gift from God.*"[41] Yes! His grace for us is the complete redemption of our sins. Nothing we can do on this earth can give us greater hope and confidence for all facets of life than the free and

---

[39] Allie Beth Stuckey, *You're Not Enough (And That's Okay): Escaping the Toxic Culture of Self-Love* (Sentinel, 2020), 154, 11.

[40] Hillary Morgan Ferrer, General Editor, *Mama Bear Apologetics: Empowering Your Kids to Challenge Cultural Lies* (Harvest House Publishers, 2019), 210.

[41] Ephesians 2:8 (NLT).

beautiful gift of God's grace. And we did nothing to earn it! It wasn't the result of some mantra we repeated over and over again as a way of positive self-talk. All credit goes to God. He gives us grace for our many failings, grace for the way we elevate ourselves above others, grace for the way we try to "fix" ourselves on our own, grace for our insecurities, and grace for our sins. Perhaps even more amazing in my mind is that we are not left in the middle of our shame, sin, and self-criticism.

God has given us not only grace but *also* hope and security in the eternal love of God through his Son, Jesus. When you consider this, the fear of what others think pales in comparison to the firm foundation of knowing that Christ is truly all we need. God doesn't want us to spend the gift of life He has given us wallowing in self-doubt, drowning in our insecurities. On the contrary, He gave us the gift of life so that we might replace our self-love with an outward expression of love toward others and, in doing so, live a full, rich, and satisfying life.[42] Scripture promises that when we give of ourselves to others, regardless of our shyness, insecurities, or fear of what others might think, but instead, trusting in the Lord to redeem our weaknesses, in return, what we receive is *"a good measure, pressed down, shaken together and running over."*[43]

---

[42] John 10:10b (NLT).
[43] Luke 6:38 (NLT).

Five

Roots

For no one can lay any foundation other than the one already laid, which is Christ Jesus.

1 Corinthians 3:11

"There are two lasting gifts we can give our children—one is roots, the other is wings." This quote was on a framed picture of two eagles soaring in the sky that hung above our couch on Babuyan Island. I can still see the red *narra* hardwood couch with a lattice rattan seat, a beautiful piece of furniture, hand-crafted by one of our Ibatan friends. To be completely honest, I can't remember exactly why this picture stuck in my mind so poignantly. Perhaps it was because it was hung in such a prominent place in our home that I saw it every day. Or perhaps I felt envious that the eagles seemed to fly so effortlessly over the treetops without any semblance of being nauseated or motion sick. Why were those big birds so settled, so content, and so comfortable high up in the atmosphere? They flew with confidence, looking strong and regal.

I have searched for the author of this quote, and there appears to be some speculation as to who originally spoke it or penned it. Some say Henry Ward Beecher, others say Jonas Salk, and still others say Hodding Carter. Regardless of who the first person was to come up with this quote, there is a deeply profound message in these few words. Roots come before wings. Roots ground our childhood, laying a foundation for our future as adults while establishing a firm footing. Roots plant us securely so that later, when we are forced to withstand strong winds and fierce rain, we are not overcome by the storm.

While my roots were physically grounded in Asia, my parents diligently strived to establish deep, spiritual roots founded in Scripture. They affirmed this in our daily family life so that no matter where we ended up living (Asia, North America, or even elsewhere), no matter what wind of difficulty blew, we could stand firm knowing that we had a strong foundation.

My childhood wasn't perfect, but my parents gave me sufficient roots so that despite my shyness and my nervousness on the big stage of life, my roots were deep enough to hold on to the truth of God's Word. In essence, this is all we need for our roots to grow. It doesn't really matter how shy I was (or how shy I still am), where I grew up, what college I went to, or even how my parents raised me. The Word of God is our firm foundation.

What I am most grateful for is that my parents introduced me to Christ and taught me the importance of reading the Word of God. *"Blessed is the one who trusts in the Lord, whose confidence is in him."*[44] From the time my sister and I were learning how to read, we were learn-

---

[44] Jeremiah 17:7 (NIV).

ing what it meant to read the Bible. Every night before bed, we had family devotions. Together as a family, we began reading aloud in Genesis, one verse at a time, and worked our way through the entire Bible, all the way to Revelation. As much as we begged my parents to skip through Leviticus and Numbers, we read every name listed in the genealogy of the Israelites! My parents were insistent that my sister and I have our own Bibles, so when were about five or six years old, we were gifted with a beautiful, leather-bound Bible, inscribed with our names on the front cover. There was ownership in this thought process. Practically, we could underline verses that meant something to us without getting our parents' permission. More importantly, however, it was personal. We were reading God's Word from our very own Bibles.

In our toddler years, my dad would read the Bible to us, paraphrasing the stories and making up songs to go with each story. Sometimes the song was the story! I didn't realize until much later in life that not everyone knew Dad's Bible songs by heart. I thought they were taken right out of some type of Bible story songbook that everyone knew about. I still know many of those songs today from memory! As we got older, we took turns reading a verse at a time until we completed the chapter. I remember when my mother decided that reading one verse wasn't enough. So we all took turns reading two verses, which ultimately turned into reading two chapters because one chapter was over too quickly! Still later, perhaps when we were in middle school and when we had begun to really speak the tribal language from Babuyan, we began to read Scripture as a family in Ibatan. We began reading one chapter each night in English and then we would read that same chapter in

Ibatan, a chapter that my parents had sometimes just finished translating. If my parents hadn't yet translated the book of the Bible we were currently reading, then we read *The Pilgrim's Progress* in Ibatan since that was a book they had translated during the early days of their time on Babuyan.

I was probably only about eight or nine years old when I began to understand, with distinct clarity, the importance of reading Scripture together as a family. It didn't matter where we were, in our home in Bagabag on the SIL Center or in our small wooden house with the thatched grass roof on Babuyan Island, we read the Bible together as a family.

I look back on those times in my childhood with fond memories. Sure as a teenager, I would roll my eyes when it came to family devotions. I would often complain and say, *"How come other kids don't have family devotions every night that last an hour?"* But in the end, I started to see that reading Scripture out loud actually had some practical payoffs. I was quick to find a passage of Scripture during Bible drills in Sunday school. If you attended a church like I did in the late 1980s and early 1990s, you might remember something called a Bible drill. Putting our Bibles over our heads, we waited for the Sunday school teacher to yell "go" before racing to see who could find the passage of scipture in question the quickest. More than that, though, I began to realize that it gave me an intimate knowledge of God's Word. Now as a grown adult with my own family, family devotions with my children are a priority, as are reading Scripture out loud and praying before bedtime.

As a preteen, I began to develop a deep interest in the Bible. I would have my own devotions throughout the week, trying to see how many chapters I could read by myself. During high school, I cherished the times I could go off on my own, sit on a grassy hill, and read God's Word, journaling my thoughts and prayers as I read. I could spend hours in nature, marveling at God's handiwork, my Bible in my lap, pen in hand.

I loved reading about the different characters in the Bible. Their stories came to life because I knew that they were real people who had lived real lives. My favorite books, however, were the minor prophets: Joel, Amos, Hosea, Micah, Nahum, and Habakkuk. Their sorrow over the sins God's people had committed and for the terrible situations they found themselves in was so apparent, and yet the love and loyalty they had for Yahweh, the God of their Fathers, ran deep and true. More importantly, God's faithful love for His people, Israel, was so evident. Despite their sin and rebellion, God always had a plan for redemption and restoration. Amid their failings, He provided hope and forgiveness.

I can't pinpoint a time in my young life when I said the sinner's prayer and accepted Jesus as my Savior, but around the age of nine or ten, I knew I was a Christian because I believed that Jesus had died to save me from my sins and that He had risen again victorious over death! As my relationship with Jesus began to grow deeper, I knew that somehow, I needed to publicly proclaim my decision to follow Christ.

Baptism was a serious discussion. My parents, of course, wanted to be sure that I understood that baptism in itself did not save me and that only the finished work of Christ's death and resurrection was what granted me eternal life with God in heaven. I suppose I understood this with my child's mind, but it wasn't until I was much older and had experienced deep heartache that I truly grasped what it meant to be a child of God. My decision to be baptized was, however, based on a firm conviction that, as a child of God and a follower of Jesus Christ who had been redeemed by his death and resurrection on the cross, I needed to be obedient to God's Word. If I wanted to follow Jesus, to really live my life for Him, then I needed to do what it said in His Word and make my commitment to follow him public.

On June 24, 1990, at ten years old, I was baptized in a freshwater spring with several other young missionary kids, including my sister. I remember the day vividly. My family, along with other SIL families, was attending our biennial conference at SIL's southern center in Nasuli, located outside the City of Malaybalay on the southern island of Mindanao. Members of SIL and Wycliffe Bible Translators would gather every two years for a two-week conference to not only discuss business matters but also to celebrate the various New Testament translations that had recently been published.

The Nasuli SIL Center was much like the Bagabag SIL Center in the northern Philippines, only this center was much larger, had many more trees, and had one coveted resource that the northern missionary kids from Bagabag were all jealous of. While the Bagabag Center had a community pool where we, as kids, spent a large amount of our time, the Nasuli Center had a beautiful, cold, freshwater spring that made the tropical afternoon heat melt away the instant you dove into the icy cold water. I'm not saying that we weren't in favor of a cold afternoon sweet treat, but if any of us hot and sweaty missionary kids were asked to choose between an ice-cream cone that might melt before we even had a chance to finish it and an afternoon at the spring, more often than not, we would have chosen the spring! We would spend hours down at the spring, racing to the wooden dock in the middle of the spring, swinging off the rope swing, or tubing down the river that flowed out of the spring.

The Sunday morning that I was baptized also happened to be John the Baptist Day. The main religion in the Philippines is Catholicism, and as a result, the *"Pista ng Bayan ng San Juan"* is a festival widely celebrated in the Philippines. This festival honors Saint John the Baptist because he was the precursor of Jesus, announcing His coming, and he baptized not only Jesus's followers but also Jesus Himself. On this day, you run the risk of being doused with a bucket of water (even strangers!) should you step outside. Many Filipinos often visit whatever body of water is closest to them and enjoy a fun "day at the beach."

The Nasuli spring is a public spring, so you can imagine how many dozens of Filipinos were celebrating in the water on this particular John the Baptist Day. I can remember the stares as they witnessed us willingly being dunked under the water in baptism, not just doused by a surprise bucket of water or pushed into the spring. There was something formal and mysterious, a sacred element encasing our baptism.

Being baptized in front of dozens of people is not necessarily unusual, particularly if you attend a large church, but what I will always remember are the faces of the Filipinos who stood on the sidelines watching. I wondered if they knew what was taking place and if they thought we were ridiculous, or if perhaps we were just taking their holiday "to the next level." Nevertheless, I remember as I stepped into the cold water that I knew I was being obedient and prayed that my baptism would be a positive testimony to whoever was watching. I believe that this significant point in my young life allowed me to put a stake in the ground of my spiritual life. My baptism was an *Ebenezer*, an altar of stones to mark a point in my life where I chose to allow the Word of God to take root in my life and cause me to step out in an act of obedience.

During difficult times in my life, I have looked back on my baptism as a definitive mark on the timeline of my life. If I ever doubted being a Christian and whether it was "worth it," I could always look back on June 24, 1990, the day I was baptized, and remember my personal decision to follow God's Word. It was a time in my life that cemented my decision to be a Christ follower. I can say then and now, with all honesty, that following Christ has always been worth it. Being rooted in God's Word has given me a lifeline when I needed it. My Bible is filled with notes, marked with dates, a record of God's faithfulness in my life, a testament to the fulfillment of His promises and His still-unfinished work in my life. While I pray that God grants me many more years on this earth, I can say with conviction and certainty that "*all my life You have been faithful. All my life You have been so, so good. With every breath that I am able Oh, I will sing of the goodness of God.*"[45]

What does it mean, then, to have roots and, if we have children, to give them roots? It means to prepare the solid, fertile ground so that their deepest beliefs, their dreams, and their fears—in short, their very identity—become firmly grounded, rooted in Christ. Some

---

[45] Bethel Music, "Goodness of God," Track #3 on *Without Words: Genesis*, Bethel Music, 2019.

thirty-odd years after my baptism, and now that I am a parent, I understand this more deeply than I ever could have before. It's true that when the storms of life batter against you and the rains of sorrow and disappointment wash over you, the type of roots you have and the depth at which they are planted determine whether you will withstand the storm.

The burden of this responsibility weighs heavily on my shoulders as I contemplate what will happen when my children are old enough to encounter the trials and hurt of adolescent and adult life. How will they respond to betrayal? How will they react when the unexpected hurt pierces their heart? Will their pain be engraved on their tombstone, or will it be used to build a bridge for others to cross over from sorrow and bitterness to joy and forgiveness? My prayer for my children is that their

> roots will grow down into God's love and keep strong. And may [they] have the power to understand, as all God's people should, how wide, how long, how high and how deep his love is. May [they] experience the love of Christ, though it is too great to understand fully. Then [they] will be made complete with all the fullness of life and power that comes from God.[46]

Solid, steady, grounded, unwavering, established, rooted—all these words depict a firm foundation. As par-

---

[46] Ephesians 3:17–19 (NLT).

ents, it is our job to provide soil rich in nutrients from Scripture. We are like gardeners who inspect for weeds, pulling out any sin that will one day choke out the little plant we are nurturing. We carefully water, at first with just a sprinkle, teaching them short prayers and Bible verses, and then, as our children grow, we add a steady stream of biblical knowledge, providing life-giving water directly from the Source of Life. We tend the soil, hoping that one day we will see growth, the greenery of new life, and later beautiful blooming flowers as the fruit of the Spirit becomes evident. It takes time and patience to guide and disciple our little ones to spiritual maturity. And yet, while we can provide roots, it is still a personal, individual decision to accept Jesus Christ as one's own Lord and Savior.

If you think about it, we are all like little children spiritually, if we have accepted Christ as our Savior, ever-growing, every deepening in our knowledge of and love for the Lord. Ironically, as our children grow, we teach them to become independent and self-reliant, but in the process of maturing and becoming more like Christ, we gradually become more dependent on him. We realize that we are incapable of anything good apart from the righteousness of Christ. Colossians 2:7 says, *"Let your roots grow down into Him, and let your lives be built on Him. Then your faith will grow strong in the truth you were taught, and you will overflow with thankfulness."*[47]

I have only been a parent for just over a decade, so I have much to learn about raising children to be Christ's followers. My inability, however, is precisely the place where God can teach me and perfect me. It will take my

---
[47] Colossians 2:7 (NLT).

whole lifetime to learn what it truly means to be a Christ follower. I pray fervently that my children will grow up to be steadfast Christ followers themselves and that one day they will be blessed with children of their own to disciple and shepherd. C. S. Lewis says that perfection is not only something God calls us to but also something He helps us attain by carrying us and picking us up when we fall, calling us to Himself until one day we are ushered into the splendor of living life eternally with Him.

> The practical up-shot is this. On the one hand, God's demand for perfection need not discourage you in the least in your present attempts to be good, or even in your present failures. Each time you fall He will pick you up again. And He knows perfectly well that your own efforts are never going to bring you anywhere near perfection. On the other hand, you must realise from the outset that the goal towards which He is beginning to guide you is absolute perfection; and no power in the whole universe, except you yourself, can prevent Him from taking you to that goal.
> We may be content to remain what we call "ordinary people": but He is determined to carry out a quite different plan.[48]

---

[48] C. S. Lewis, *Mere Christianity* (Glasgow: Fount, 1997), 167–168.

We can certainly go through life adding a list of successes to our résumé, or conversely, stacking up our failures as a reminder of how we will never measure up. Truly, the goal of our lives, however, is to honor God in all aspects of our lives, regardless of the accomplishments or fiascos we may experience. Both our triumphs and defeats mold us and shape us into who God longs for and intends us to be. We know that we will never be truly complete and whole until we are one day made new and perfect when we see Him face-to-face, but that does not stop us from striving to honor Him to the best of our abilities until that glorious and long-expected day comes.

> If we let Him—for we can prevent Him, if we choose—He will make the feeblest and filthiest of us into a god or goddess, a dazzling, radiant, immortal creature, pulsating all through with such energy and joy and wisdom and love as we cannot now imagine, a bright stainless mirror which reflects back to God perfectly (though of course, on a smaller scale), His own boundless power and delight and goodness.[49]

How utterly freeing it is to know that our failures are not our ultimate defeat. The very fact that we strive to be the perfect parent, the perfect spouse, and the perfect friend shows our very imperfect nature. We cannot achieve perfection in any one of these categories, and yet

---
[49] C. S. Lewis, *Mere Christianity*, 170.

we are still called to the highest standard of perfection. And here is the paradox. In the midst of this apparent impossibility, our feeble minds, our desperate failures, and our incompleteness are not wasted. Instead, they are used to lead us to a place where we know we are nothing without Christ.

C. S. Lewis goes on to say, "*The process will be long and in parts very painful, but that is what we are in for. Nothing less...He meant what He said. Those who put themselves in His hands will become perfect, as He is perfect—perfect in love, wisdom, joy, beauty and immortality.*"[50] What a promise to cling to!

In our desperate moments, when we have depleted all our attempts at success and when we seem to be at the end of our abilities, our strength, and our determination, we are not alone. Whether you are married, single, have children, or are desperately waiting for the day you can hold your own child in your arms, your disaster stories, your failures, your victories, and your sorrows do not go unseen. You are immeasurably more than your defeat. You are exceedingly loved, valued for who you are as a child of God, cherished, and precious. In fact, you were so highly esteemed and so priceless that the cost for you, for me, was Christ's death on the cross. That is your worth. That is the exorbitant love of the Father for us that He would give his only Son for our redemption.[51]

As I write this, my entire family is asleep, and I am alone with my thoughts in a dark and quiet house. It is the end of a very long day, and I sit in silence and review the events of the past sixteen or so hours. Could I

---

[50] C. S. Lewis, *Mere Christianity*, 170–171.
[51] John 3:16.

have been a more patient mother to my children? (We all know the answer to this rhetorical question. A profound "Yes!") Could I have spoken with more kindness to my husband? (Again, the answer to this rhetorical question is the same as the first.) Could I have meditated more on God's Word? What could I have done differently? How should I have responded differently? Why didn't I say that with more gentleness?

The end of the day can overwhelmingly look like a pile of dirty laundry that somehow never ceases to grow smaller; a multitude of failures stacked up and towering over your hard efforts at patience, kindness, and love; and a list of unanswered questions that continually barrage you and constantly nag at the back of your mind. And so we have a choice. We can choose to see our life like a pile of dirty laundry, or we can choose to see, in the last remaining moments of the day, a reflection of God's goodness—His faithfulness in carrying us through the events of such a long day, despite whatever failures or disappointments we may have encountered. We can celebrate His grace and goodness for us even when we don't deserve it.

Scripture is full of passages that speak of God's faithfulness and provision. Lamentations 3:22 says, *"Because of the LORD's great love we are not consumed, for His compassions never fail. They are new every morning; great is your faithfulness."*[52] How grateful I am that each morning is literally a new day! You might overlook this in the business of life we often call the "rat race." But truly, tomorrow is a brand-new day, a fresh start, a redo of sorts, and God's faithfulness to us is renewed each morning. As the

---
[52] Lamentations 3:22 (NIV).

sun rises on a new day, we are given a fresh ray of hope, a glimmer of something eternally new, untainted by disappointment, unmarred by grief or turmoil. In essence, a glimpse of perfection.

Being rooted, grounded, and firmly established in the Word of God means that we are not overcome by life's trials. We can claim the promise of eternal life[53] because when we are richly planted in the soil of God's Word, we can awake with hope and vigor, knowing that *"as far as the east is from the west, so far has he removed our transgressions from us."*[54] We then have confidence for whatever we need to face because we *"know that the LORD [our] God is God; he is the faithful God, keeping his covenant of love to a thousand generations of those who love him and keep his commandments."*[55] We can rely on God's Word as truth. We can trust that God will remain faithful to his Word, drawing us to Him, and will continue to perfect us until the day that we will live forever with Him in glory.

---

[53] 1 John 2:25 (NIV).
[54] Psalm 103:12 (NIV).
[55] Deuteronomy 7:9 (NLT).

Six

Wings

But those who hope in the Lord will renew their strength, they will soar on wings like eagles.

Isaiah 40:31a

Babies are so sweet, so precious, so adorable and squishy. I'm sure at some point, if you have children, you have told them to "stop growing!" because we want our children to stay forever cute and cuddly, to always want them to snuggle with us and hold our hands. If we are honest, we don't want them to grow up because it is quite possible that once they are independent and self-sufficient, they may not need us anymore. That is a fear I certainly face as a parent. "What if they don't need me?" "What if someone else can fill the role that I have played as their mother for so long?"

We all want to feel wanted, needed, and looked up to by others, and we certainly want our children to need us. (I love it when my children run to me with open arms so that I can fix their boo-boos, wipe their tears, and reassure them that I will always be there for them. Of course, I am helping meet a physical need for my child at this point, but at the same time, I am also getting an emotional need of my own met.) We want to teach our children things that we know and watch their eyes sparkle as they look at us with awe, knowing that we are their whole world.

We tell ourselves that we will miss folding their never-ending mounds of tiny washed clothes; making little lunches for every school day; driving them to little league, gymnastics, and soccer; and mustering up a forced laugh for their ridiculous, made-up jokes that make no sense. And then, of course, we also remember all those sleepless nights, the cluster feedings, pumping schedules, trying to get work done with children who refuse to take a nap, hair and house a mess, and a host of other tremendously difficult tasks that demand our attention during a twenty-four-hour period (with very little sleep). All those things, however, we would do over again in a heartbeat for our children because we love them.

Not too long ago, my son, who was seven years old at the time, had a bad dream and came to crawl into bed with me. I was already having a rough night, having rearranged everyone's sleeping situations because of my husband being sick. My daughter, who was eight years old at the time, was now sleeping in my son's room, sharing his double bed so that I could sleep in my daughter's bed and give my husband a better night's sleep in our room. (Talk about a juggling act! Who was in which bed now?) And please don't go thinking that I am a "sweet wife." I mean, I am for the most part, but I also didn't want to get sick! So shoving my daughter's plethora of stuffed animals aside, I climbed up into her bunkbed and hunkered down for the night. At 4:30 a.m., the sound of the creaking bunkbed stairs woke me as my son climbed up them to tell me his bad dream had made him scared. I put my arms around him as he worked his way under the covers and snuggled up next to me. I kissed his head and prayed for him to have a good sleep and that his mind wouldn't be bothered anymore by bad dreams. I heard his breathing even out as he quickly fell back to sleep, thanking the Lord for this precious time with my son. I knew that soon he would grow out of wanting to crawl into bed at night and cuddle up with me.

At about four forty-five, the thought occurred to me that I was exceedingly uncomfortable. My husband was fast asleep, alone, in a king-size bed. I could hear my daughter snoring away blissfully in the next room, alone in a double bed. Meanwhile, my son and I were sharing a twin-sized mattress on a bunk bed that barely had enough room for me, never mind my growing son and a large family of dolls, unicorns, squishmallows, teddy bears, and beanie boos. (I'm not sure when the last time was that you may have slept on the top bunk of a bunk bed, but the ceiling is awfully close!) At four forty-six, my son was back in the double bed with my daughter, and I spent the last few hours rather unsuccessfully trying to get back to sleep.

While we want our children to always need us and to come to us when they want to feel safe, we certainly don't want them to be entirely dependent on us for the rest of their adult lives. The reality is that we don't actually want a forty-year-old child living with us and snuggling up next to us at night, do we? That would truly cross over from precious to absurd and downright awkward. There is a natural process to growing up, and as good parents, we, of course, want our children to become healthy adults who are productive members of society.

There is, obviously, no easy formula that we can follow as parents to ensure this successful transition from childhood through adolescence and eventually to adulthood. With solid roots, however, a firm biblical foundation, a strong family allegiance, and a thriving relationship with the Lord Jesus, I believe that this can happen. We truly can help them establish deep roots so that when it is time, they will be able to spread their wings with confidence.

As a missionary kid, I was given the opportunity to spread my wings in my early teens; an opportunity that I may not have been able to take advantage of had my parents chosen to stay in North America instead of moving to the Philippines. My elementary schooling was completed at a small (and when I say small, I truly mean small since the total student body was around twenty-five!) missionary school at the SIL Bagabag Center. My sister and I walked to and from school each day, which took about ten to fifteen minutes (depending on if we went the long way through the gully or took the shortcut across the pond bridge).

High school, however, was a completely different ordeal. At the age of thirteen, I "went away" to boarding school. I realize that other missionary families may have sent their children to boarding school at an even earlier age than thirteen; however, as a parent of a young daughter myself, I am only now realizing the magnitude of my parents' decision to send not only me but also my sister, who was nearly two years older than me, off to boarding school at the same time. As it happens, they had planned it this way, sending us both off together, so that we wouldn't be alone and could take care of each other.

My parents lived about eight to ten hours away from the nearest international school in the Philippines that offered a North American curriculum, and one that would be accredited and accepted by universities in both Canada and the United States. As Wycliffe Bible Translators, they were committed to translating the Scriptures for a remote people group. Every few months, we would travel to Babuyan Island (approximately two hours away via the small Helio Courier, a single-prop airplane) for them to learn the language, translate Scripture, and get to know the people. For them to do that, they needed to live close enough to the SIL Bagabag Center where the JAARS pilots were located so that they could fly there (going by land and sea could take upward of a week because of the distance, as well as possible choppy seas that the small outrigger boats would be unable to navigate).

Manila, the capital city of the Philippines where the international school was located, was too far away from the SIL Bagabag Center. And so, Faith Academy, a Christian school for K–12 that taught both the US and European (IGCSE) curriculums, was our only option for high school other than being homeschooled or attending a local Filipino school that only went as far as grade ten. When given the choice, both my sister and I asked to be sent to Faith Academy rather than continue traveling with my parents and having to be homeschooled. This required us to live in a dorm on campus. At the time, Faith Academy was the largest Christian international boarding school in Asia.

These were some of the best years of my adolescent life. It was here that I learned to push myself out of my tiny shell of shyness to try new and adventurous things. I somehow mustered up enough courage during my freshman year to try out for the volleyball team. I became a co-captain on the JV team as a freshman, made varsity my junior year, and then competed with my team in Japan at the Far East Volleyball Tournament my senior year. I learned to see past my anxiety and step outside my comfort zone to direct our junior class Talent Night, act in our senior class play, and become the student council secretary. I also knew that pushing myself academically would help me as I applied for North American colleges, so I took as many math, science, and AP classes that my schedule could accommodate.

My time at Faith Academy cemented my conviction that Jesus truly had saved and redeemed me. He was with me, carrying me through those years. He carries me still. I knew that because the Lord had been faithful to me during my time in boarding school, away from my parents, that He would continue to be faithful as I moved on to college. I remember asking God to help me, to stay by me as I moved into the uncharted territory of postsecondary education where I would be attending university in a foreign country (known as Canada). What would I encounter there? While I knew it would be an adventure I must somehow figure out how to navigate, I was certain that God would meet me wherever I was, even if it happened to be a place in the in-between, a place of limbo and uncertainty. Through the successes and failures and the excitements and disappointments I experienced in high school, I learned that He is constant. He is enough.

Of course, it was difficult to be away from my parents for such long stretches of time while I was so young, but living in a dorm with twenty-two other girls means you are truly never alone! Finding a quiet space to myself was often literally impossible! During my first year at Faith Academy, I was assigned to a small room with three other freshman girls. This was my second time being a freshman! (The year before, my parents had taken a furlough year in British Columbia, Canada. This furlough year is required by SIL/WBT for all missionaries every four to five years to allow them to return to their home countries and reacquaint themselves with family and friends and continue to raise both prayer and financial support partners. British Columbia's education system includes eighth grade as high school, and so because I entered eighth grade that year, I was considered a freshman.) After returning from furlough in Canada, I attended Faith Academy as a dorm student. At Faith Academy, I was a freshman again, this time, for ninth grade.

The room we were assigned to was located on the third floor of one of the three on-campus dorms. It was simple and furnished with only what was necessary. There were two sets of bunkbeds in each dorm room, four small closets, and two desks that doubled as vanities. The dorm consisted of six rooms, very similar to the one I was in, and two bathrooms, each with two stalls and two showers (with no hot water!). It was a miracle, but somehow, all twenty-two of us girls (one year, there were twenty-three girls) managed to shower and get ready for school on time each day. School started at 7:25 a.m.

The middle floor consisted of the dorm parents' apartment (private living quarters for their family), the kitchen, dining room, and common living area. The dining room was at the end of a large room and had four or five large square tables where we ate our meals together and did homework. The living area was on the other end of the room. We rarely hung out in this space because it was more like an entryway since it was close to the front door and only had a few seats. The stairs going up to our bedrooms were also here, so it served more as a passageway between rooms.

Just outside the dorm parents' apartment was the telephone. This old, heavy, black rotary phone was our lifeline to our parents and our friends outside the dorm. It sat on a stand at the top of the stairs that led to the basement. You could often hear girls talking in various languages to their parents and other family members or friends on the phone.

Sitting on the stairs halfway down to the basement with the lights turned off and speaking a language we knew the others weren't familiar with, we at least had the illusion of privacy. This tiny space in the middle of the stairs created a space to bridge our world of school, friends, and dorm life with our parents' faraway world of Bible translation and linguistic research. Unfortunately, for my sister and me, the island on which our parents spent most of their time did not have a phone. Often, the only communication we received from them was in the form of a radio message that was broadcast during their regular morning roll calls, received by the head SIL/Wycliffe Office in Manila, and then sent by mail on the bus to our school. Needless to say, we were not always up to date on the most current information regarding my parents, and vice versa.

The basement held another common living area. This is where we had dorm devotions and where we went to study or work on collaborative school projects such as artwork, group presentations, or other such assignments. It was also quite a few degrees cooler in the basement. Without air-conditioning, any chance to study in the basement was a welcome opportunity. I can recall countless hours spent drawing or doing homework on the cold cement floor, my sweaty hands leaving marks on the paper. The basement also included space for the laundry room, a guest room for parents, the house helpers' living area, the piano, the one and only desktop computer, and a printer. Just imagine twenty-two girls and one computer to type reports, essays, and other school assignments. It was a masterful feat of scheduling to get all our assignments typed and printed on time. (And don't forget, this was during the mid-1990s when laser inkjet printers were still expensive. We were still using a dot matrix printer, so you can imagine not only how long it took to print an eight-page essay but also how loud it was!)

Practicing piano was another monumental task. While not all twenty-two girls took piano lessons, there were typically at least four or five girls who did, and it was nearly impossible for all of us to practice daily. Fortunately, our dorm had an acoustic piano (ancient as it might have been), so at least we weren't practicing on a miniature keyboard as I had done in my early childhood years! Somehow, though, we all managed to get some practice during the week, although I have great sympathy for our piano teacher, Mrs. Carol Kuiken (whom we affectionately called "Aunt Carol"), who must have heard our same songs repeatedly for lack of practice!

Aunt Carol was also a missionary with SIL/WBT. She and her husband, who taught fifth grade at Faith Academy, lived close to the Faith Academy campus and had children who attended Faith Academy. Out of the generosity of her heart, Aunt Carol offered piano lessons for free to any missionary kid at Faith Academy who wanted lessons.

Not only was Aunt Carol my piano teacher, she and her family were also my guardians. My parents specifically chose the Kuiken family to be guardians for me and my sister during our high school years because of their kindness, their fun family atmosphere, and also because their home was located close to the Faith Academy campus. Since we were dorm students, the Kuikens were our official "stand-in parents" in case of an emergency, but more importantly, their home was always open to us whenever we needed a break from dorm life. I am deeply grateful to Uncle Bob and Aunt Carol and their family for their friendship over the years and for not only listening to our piano pieces dozens of times (I'm sure even Uncle Bob knew our pieces by heart he had heard them so many times!) but also for their sacrificial love for us during those dorm-life years.

While quarters were a little cramped, living in a dorm certainly taught me how to share. The blessing of living with twenty-two other "sisters" meant that you had twenty-two other closets to browse through in the morning. On the flip side, it was often hard to keep track of who had borrowed your clothes! We were responsible for our own toiletries; however, if you ran out of shampoo, there was always someone willing to let you use theirs if, on the next shopping trip, you bought them an extra bottle. There was typically someone available to help you with a difficult math problem or explain a homework assignment that didn't make sense. With twenty-two girls in one house, there were plenty of people to talk to if you needed advice on anything (although sometimes you got more advice than you asked for!). More than that, though, this little community of "dormies" created a unique place of belonging for us girls living between childhood and adulthood, far from our parents and way of life at home. The dorm life was a different "home away from home" that we all adapted to, first out of necessity and then out of routine and familiarity.

In general, it was a positive experience living in a dorm full of girls. I wasn't always best friends with every girl, but overall, some of my longest-lasting friends were girls who lived in my dorm. Dorm life bonded us "dormies" together. We all had something in common: Our parents were far away, and so we became family whether we liked it or not. Faith Academy even built in an extra week during the school year for each dorm to bond together on vacation, typically at a beach resort. This was called "Family Weekend." Our dorm would pile up in the school van or *Tamaraw* (a Filipino hybrid vehicle that looked like a cross between a truck and an SUV with open sides), and would make our way through Manila traffic, squished together side by side like hens huddled up for the cold, except it was blazing hot inside the *Tamaraw* because there was no air-conditioning.

Because the seats were merely benches that ran lengthwise on either side of the vehicle (and there were certainly no seat belts), we piled our luggage on the floor in the middle of the benches, resting our feet on top of them. The smells of the city smog and traffic seeped into our crowded ride and lingered like a haze in the midst of us. We would ride in the car for several hours south (depending on how bad the traffic was) to the dock to take the ferry to Puerto Galera on Mindoro Island (the seventh largest island in the Philippines, located in the central island portion of the Philippines, off the southwestern coast of Luzon). We would arrive hot, tired, cranky, and hungry but filled with excitement to be at the beach for a week.

We had dreamed of fresh green mango shakes, *calamansi* juice in tall glasses (sort of like a cross between lemonade and limeade), and fried rice dished out in little mounds on our plates. At the end of the week, we would be sunburned and relaxed, sad to trade in our little huts on the beach for the smog and busy streets of Manila. For a final treat on the journey back, we would stop at McDonald's for burgers and hot fudge sundaes. We all looked forward to Family Weekend, and I am thankful to our dorm parents who made the effort each year to take twenty-two teenage girls (all ex-patriots, or "expats") to a beach and bring them all back safely!

While all of us girls had parents who lived far away, my sister and I were fortunate that we only had to take a ten-hour bus ride home to see our parents. Other girls' parents lived in China, Indonesia, or Thailand, and travel was obviously quite costly for them when they wanted to see their parents. For the most part, however, most of us dormies only saw our parents over Christmas break and summer vacation.

The bus ride that my sister and I took to get home over these breaks was an experience that terrified me because we were alone, without the supervision of an adult, and it was such a long, uncomfortable ride with complete strangers. While we spoke some Tagalog (the national language of the Philippines), we weren't completely fluent and were forced to use a mixture of English and Tagalog, called *Taglish*, when speaking to the conductor or other passengers. *Taglish*, by the way, is an official term used by Filipinos to describe what they commonly use themselves when speaking to foreigners like us who didn't quite know the language well enough to pass for natives.

Once we got farther north in our journey, our limited *Taglish* didn't really help us very much because the main language used in the northern part of the Philippines is Ilocano, and neither of us spoke that, other than a few phrases we had picked up here and there. Fortunately, we always had each other and never had to make the trip alone.

At Christmas break, our dorm dad would drive us to the busy Baliwag bus station on Edsa Street in the bustling metropolis of Manila. Tickets in hand, we would board the "air-con" bus (my parents paid extra so we could have air-conditioning and our own seats instead of sitting in the aisle), piling our luggage on top of our laps. If we got there early enough, we didn't have to sit in the back. Although my sister and I would switch seats periodically, I typically got the seat next to the window, in case I had to throw up.

Without cell phones, my parents would have to calculate the time it would take the bus to travel north from Manila to the drop-off point, called *Junction* just outside the little town of Bagabag. They would meet us there and drive us the last ten minutes home, down the gravel road to the SIL Center where our childhood home was.

The bus had scheduled stops en route for passengers to use the restroom and buy snacks and included one longer stop for lunch. Sticking together, my sister and I never left anything valuable on the bus. Our luggage remained, but anything else of importance came with us, including toilet paper. We learned from experience that you must always bring your own toilet paper with you to a public restroom. (Toilet paper can be in the form of the actual roll, which is far too cumbersome to travel with, or preferably a pack of Kleenex that you can easily shove in your purse or pocket.)

As in North America, bus stations are not typically the most sought-after restrooms, but on these journeys north, it was our only option, aside from a bush on the side of the road. Using the restroom, or "comfort room," as it is referred to in the Philippines, is notably an endeavor you want to complete in the shortest amount of time possible! Often, in the rural parts of the Philippines, there is no toilet to use but rather a stall with a hole in the ground. If there is a bucket of water to use for flushing, you are in business!

The lunch stop was always a little more pleasant as the restrooms were cleaner, and the stop was a little longer. My sister and I would share something to eat, usually, some sort of Filipino dish of rice and chicken if we were very hungry. If nothing looked too appetizing, we opted for *pandesal*, a type of Filipino bread roll, or other snacks such as *chicharon* (fried pork fat chips), a bag of *Chippy*s (similar to Fritos), *Boy Bawang Cornik* corn nuts, or *Nagaraya* cracker nuts. Sometimes we would splurge and share a freshly made *biko* (sweet sticky rice cake) or *suman* (sticky rice with coconut and caramel wrapped in banana leaves). It was a special treat for us when we got to eat sticky rice as we didn't have it very often in the dorm. A little bit of that sugary sticky rice at a bus stop gave us just enough willpower to climb back onto the crowded bus for another long haul before we would be able to stop to stretch our legs and breathe in fresh air once again.

(Before moving to the dorm, while living at the SIL Bagabag Center, we had looked forward to Manang[56] Ligaya, the "Sticky Rice Lady," as we affectionately called her, who would walk to the center from the neighboring town, her rice winnower full of sticky rice covered with a large banana leaf to keep the flies away. All the kids at the center ran over to her with what coins they had to buy sticky rice. Sometimes she even had banana cue—grilled bananas covered in a sticky caramel sugar glaze on a stick. She sold out quickly, so if you didn't get there in time, you would have to wait until the next time she came for a bite of her delicious treats. The "Sticky Rice Lady" and her afternoon snacks were a magnet for kids and grown-ups alike, just like the ice-cream truck that slowly drives down your street on a hot summer day.)

After several stops, ten hours in a crowded bus, and bumpy, windy roads through the mountains (known as Dalton Pass) to Nueva Vizcaya Province, we were ready to be home. It was truly a miracle that, somehow, without cell phones or online tracking, our parents were always on time to meet us at the *Junction*.

My parents certainly gave us wings early on in our adolescent years, allowing us to develop our maturity and giving us the freedom to make our own decisions. Knowing that their children were rooted in Scripture and had both accepted Jesus as their Lord and Savior before

---

[56] A term of respect for an older woman, meaning "older sister."

heading off to boarding school, I'm sure, helped ease the pain of us leaving, but I know it could not have been easy for them. I have a young daughter, and I cannot imagine putting my daughter on a ten-hour bus ride in a foreign country at the age of fourteen or fifteen, never mind sending her off to boarding school at thirteen!

As our children get older, they naturally require less assistance from us. Learning to ride a bike, to tie their shoes, or to poop in the potty seemed to be such monumental tasks at first but now are commonplace (thankfully!). My preteens no longer need help accomplishing these tasks, as they have now mastered them on their own. But what we tend to forget is that our children still need guidance. As Christians, we are called to "make disciples,"[57] to share the good news of the Gospel of Christ and to teach others to worship God in spirit and in truth.[58] Is this any different as parents, or more importantly, as Christian parents? Are we not called to make disciples, even of our own children?

What does it mean to disciple our children? Deuteronomy 11:18 says that we are to *"fix (the words of God) in your hearts and minds; tie them as reminders on your hands and bind them to your foreheads."* It is slightly impractical to walk around with small Bibles tied to our heads and hands, but the imagery is powerful. We should know God's Word so well that it is foremost on our minds—at our fingertips to use, speak, guide, and instruct. We are to *"teach them to (our) children, speaking about them when you sit at home and when you walk along the road, when you lie down and when you get up."*[59] God's

---
[57] Matthew 28:19–20 (NLT).
[58] John 4:24 (NLT).
[59] Deuteronomy 11:18–19 (NLT).

Word should be part of our daily lives, our daily routines, and our daily events, not shoved to the sidelines for weekend Sunday services. Weaving the Word of God into our everyday lives creates a pattern of thankfulness and a culture of gratefulness as we continually look upward and outward at the situations and people God has called us to disciple.

Each morning on the way to school, my husband takes a moment to read the verse of the day and to pray out loud for our family and, specifically, for our children. They know that they can ask us to pray for anything, from a sore tummy to a big test at school. One day, we were a little rushed to get out the door. As we approached the school, my son asked, "Dad, what about the verse of the day?" I love that prayer and Scripture have become so engrained in our morning routine that when we are faulty as parents and become overwhelmed by the chaos of the moment, our children often bring us back to what matters most.

The truth of God's Word is not meant to be lived out in private. In Jesus's prayer for His disciples, moments before He is arrested, He pleads for the Father to "*sanctify them by the truth; your word is truth.*"[60] He asks that "*they be brought to complete unity to let the world know that you sent (him), and have loved them, even as you have loved (him).*"[61] The truth of God's never-ending love for us is paramount for our children to understand what it means to be a disciple. While our human minds are incapable of fully grasping the magnitude of the cross and the empty

---

[60] John 17:17 (NIV).
[61] John 17:23b (NIV).

tomb, something is stirred in our hearts at the very mention of the name of Jesus.

The words of God are truth and life. Jesus Himself says, "*These are written that you may believe that Jesus is the Christ, the Son of God, and that by believing you may have life in his name.*"[62] This is the call to discipleship. This is the crux of what it means to be a follower of Christ. We believe He is the Son of God and that He died for us and rose again, and because of that, we have eternal life in Him. Why would we not want our children to know this overwhelming good news and the incomparable joy that it brings?

> We will not hide them from their children but will declare to the next generation the praises of the Lord and His might, and the wonders He has performed...that the coming generation would know them—even children yet to be born—to arise and tell their own children.[63]

Children love to be included in family events. When we develop a pattern of incorporating Scripture into our family life, meditating not only on the obedience that God has called us to but also on the goodness, grace, and faithfulness of God, it creates a family bond that is not easily broken. Scripture calls us to "testify to the truth," if indeed we have the Spirit of Truth in us, not to hide it or speak it in private.[64] The truth is that

---
[62] John 20:31 (NIV).
[63] Psalm 78:4, 6 (NIV).
[64] John 15:27 (NIV).

we are full of sin, but God, in His great love for us, sent Jesus to die a gruesome death on the cross for us. And it does not end there. He calls us righteous, free of guilt and sin, because he condemned the prince of this world, rose from the dead, and granted us eternal life with Him if we choose to believe. That is the truth that we declare to our children![65]

As I think about the roots my parents gave me, a family life rich in love and grounded in the Word of God, and the wings that I was able to use, I see the fulfillment of Scripture. Just as they did not *"hide (the truth of God's Word) from their children,"* so now I am *"declar(ing) to the next generation the praises of the Lord."*[66] It is my prayer that my children, *"the coming generation,"* would in turn *"arise and tell their own children."*[67]

---

[65] John 16:11 (NIV).
[66] Psalm 78:4a (NIV).
[67] Psalm 78:6 (NIV).

Seven

Night Flight

*And hope does not put us to shame,
because God's love has been poured
out into our hearts through the Holy
Spirit, who has been given to us.*

Romans 5:5

I was seven years old when typhoon *Pepang* (Pee-pung) hit the small island of Babuyan Claro. Located in the Luzon Strait, Babuyan Claro is the northernmost island in the group of Babuyan Islands, south of Taiwan and the Philippine Batanes Islands. Because of the location of the Babuyan and Batanes Islands, severe typhoons are known to wreak havoc among this chain of islands. With winds reaching over two hundred kilometers per hour (over 125 miles per hour), *Pepang* was later referred to as the strongest typhoon the Ibatan had ever experienced. It was even considered stronger than typhoon *Miding* (Me-ding), which had devastated the island the year before and had, at that time, been known as the strongest typhoon to hit the island in living memory.

Pepang outdid *Miding* for several reasons. But the most significant, perhaps, was that it came at night. According to my mother's meticulous records, the gusty winds started to pick up in the late afternoon on Thursday, October 22, 1987. It was typhoon season, and as my mother commented, *"No one thought much if it. By the evening, the winds had amplified in strength and frequency—but winds always sound worse at night, and surely by morning, things would calm down."*[68] This was not the case. The next morning, the gusts of wind increased in frequency and intensity.

That day, JAARS had scheduled a flight to Babuyan as a quick stopover on their way to the Batanes Islands to pick up two Japanese linguists. We had been looking forward to this flight because our schoolteacher in Bagabag was going to send us a care package: a special meal of lasagna and, most importantly and my favorite, chocolate cupcakes. As you can imagine, the flight was canceled because of inclement weather, and my sister and I, not to mention my parents, were disappointed. In fact, the winds had increased so much that my mother recorded, *"Each gust of wind was like a hammer driving nails into the boards of our house."*

The wooden tree boards that made the walls of our house were merely nailed together side by side and were certainly not insulated. The wind investigated every crack and pushed with a vengeance, forcing its way into our home and creating drafts throughout the house.

We started to realize that the thatched grass roof was no match for the malicious wind. At 11:00 a.m., on Friday, October 23, my mother noted that *"the girls and*

---

[68] Judith Maree, *Personal Journal Entry*, November 1987.

I saw the southeast corner of the roof lift up." My dad and Orlando, our Ibatan friend, and my parents' primary translation partner were able to quickly tie down the roof. However, throughout the day, it was apparent that we would need to pack some things away in the *bodega*. The *bodega* was a small room near the front of our house that had a combined function of an indoor bathroom and storage facility. It was the strongest part of the house, made with tongue and groove boards, unlike the rest of the house. As the wind grew stronger, my parents also decided that it would be a good, precautionary measure to pack the medicines and other medical supplies into forty-four-gallon metal drums (such as the ones I remember in our *bodega*).

When we were living on the mainland, we stored our belongings in the locked *bodega* so that the rest of the house could be used by others if necessary. (The memories I have of this *bodega* include some wooden shelving lined with a few canned goods, papers, books and clothing, some stacked boxes and metal barrels that we used for storage, and a white ceramic toilet without a seat that had to be flushed with a bucket of water. Over the toilet was a sign that read, "If it's yellow, let it mellow; if it's brown, flush it down!")

By lunch time, the mango tree in our front yard had fallen, narrowly missing our balcony, and the *"wind was now driving the rain into the house between the cracks of each board, wetting all our beds in the northern part of the house."* My mother records that when she and my dad had to go outside, they *"became increasingly more frightened by the force of the wind. On several occasions, we'd[they'd] run and cling to each other to avoid being separated."*

In a letter sent to our supporters after the typhoon was over, my mother writes, *"Each gust of wind shook the house, and new leaks were beginning here and there. Twice the wind picked up the eastern balcony sliding door and sent it flying to our neighbor's yard."* After retrieving the balcony door for the second time, my dad decided it was time to push the alert tone on the radio to call the SIL office on the mainland, *"SIL Bagabag! SIL Bagabag! This is SIL Babuyan. We're losing our roof!"* The only thing left to do was to stay away from the windows in case any branches came crashing through, secure the roof, and wait out the storm.

I don't remember all the details of what happened in that time of waiting, but I understood the severity of the events taking place around us and knew that, if my parents gave us instructions, we would need to follow them immediately. We were obviously wide awake, with no chance of sleeping. My mother says that they tried to keep me and my sister calm by playing games, reading, and singing "Be Still and Know That I Am God," but I know there must have been fear in their hearts as they kept a constant eye on the roof, wondering if we would make it through the night. Darkness came, and the winds grew stronger.

> We didn't dare light the pressure lantern as it grew dark. I tried to prepare supper while Rundell and I took all the rope we had to secure the roof. The flame just wouldn't stay on the pot of rice I was cooking. After a quick supper of rice and beans, we packed everything away and tried to

> get the girls down to bed. The only dry place in the house was right in the middle of the dining table, so we laid our mattress on the floor [under the table] and told them to lie down. Meanwhile, Rundell and I stood guard with our flashlights, searching for any loose part of the roof. As a section lifted, Rundell ran and hammered in a nail or secured it with rope. At 7:30 p.m., Rundell, in a serious tone said, "We better have a contingency plan. Pack some warm clothes for the girls and get ready to leave if we have to."

We realized our house was about to be torn apart when our neighbor, Nemecio, pounded on our door at around 8:00 p.m. As my dad went out to let him in, a large branch from the narra tree in our front yard come crashing down within feet of where he and Nemecio were standing. At the same time, a huge section of our grass roof blew off and nearly knocked my dad to the floor. My mother writes,

> Taking hold of our fear, we all got into our raincoats and boots, grabbed our flashlights and a bag with extra batteries, a blanket and sweaters. Hastily, we padlocked the door and watched for a lull in the wind to dash across to Nemecio's house, 50 yards away. As we ran,

pushed and pulled by the wind and dodging flying branches, I stepped into a hole and twisted my ankle but managed to keep on running.

I vividly recall the flight into the darkness that night. I remember thinking that our raincoats were not doing much good, as we were already completely soaked to the bone from the pounding rain. The wind was so strong that it was difficult to stand up, never mind running through a grove of trees that seemed like a never-ending jungle, dodging all kinds of flying debris. I can only imagine my parents' adrenaline, holding fast to our hands, defying the wind that tried to rip us out of their grip. There was no time to look back. I applaud my mother's bravery, racing through the jungle on a sprained ankle, knowing that the safety of our neighbor's house was our only chance at survival.

We arrived at Nemecio's house, battered by the wind, and drenched by the rain, terrified, and exhausted, but grateful to squeeze behind the board that served as a door to his house. Nemecio had not yet finished building his house, so the lower floor was still dirt. His wife and four children, along with a schoolteacher who had made his way to Nemecio's house, made room for us as we huddled together, shivering and trying to stay warm. We kept our raincoats on, hoping they would keep us dry, because even inside the house, we were constantly being sprayed as the wind forced the rain through the tongue and groove-slatted boards. None of us cared that we had to dig a hole in the dirt floor of the house whenever we needed to use the bathroom. We were just thankful to be together, safely out of the vicious wind and driving rain. The deafening wind made it difficult for us to hear one another, although there wasn't really a lot to say. We prayed in whispers, pleading with the Lord for His protection, and that the roof on this house would hold!

I remember that at some point during that long night, all the men in the house began shouting. The wooden shutter covering the window had been torn off by the wind, and as the wind entered the house, the roof had begun to lift. Together, the men grabbed the kitchen table and threw it up against the window, nailing it in place to cover the opening. The quick reactions of the men saved the house and all of us that night. Once the table had been nailed into place, the men reinforced it with two ten-foot posts to hold it in place. After that, we kept our eyes glued to the roof, knowing that at any moment we might see a corner of it lift up and fly away.

Toward midnight, two other families arrived, completely drenched, covered in mud and grime, and wide-eyed with fear. Their terrifying flight from the seacoast, where their house had been smashed to pieces, to where we were, nearly a kilometer inland, made the hair on our arms stand up. With seven children and an infant, they ran in between gusts. When the next gust of wind started up, they threw themselves flat on the ground so that they wouldn't be picked up and thrown by the wind. By this time, the winds had increased to about 240 kilometers an hour. It was a miracle that all of them made it to Nemecio's house. We welcomed them into the crowded home, thankful that there was another man to help hold down the roof.

By seven the next morning, the winds were still as strong as ever. The morning, however, brought light and a renewed sense of hope that, although the winds were still gusting one to two minutes apart, the typhoon would soon pass by us. My mom records with humor that "like Noah, Nemecio opened a crack of the north window and looked across the road." What he saw through the crack in the window was devastating to us all. The school, just across the dirt road from Nemecio's house, had lost its roof, and there was no telling what damage had occurred on the inside of the cement walls. As Nemecio kept peering out through the small crack, he said in disbelief to my dad, "Older Brother, your house is gone!" There was no house to be seen, but only scattered remnants of a structure. It was complete rubble. My dad and Nemecio decided to brave the storm and investigate the damage. The only safe way out of the house was to squeeze through a small opening they had made in the wall, just barely enough space for one person to shimmy their way through.

You can imagine how alarming it was to see our dad crawl through the wall into the howling wind and rain. At some point, however, both my dad and Nemecio returned, unscathed, and with a few treasures. My dad had found his glasses! It only had one lens, but he was thrilled to take out his contacts for a time as they had been in for over eighteen hours at that point. Nemecio had also found the battery-operated radio! We could call for help! They reported that "it appeared that the house had been taken apart piece by piece" and that the *bodega*, the strongest part of the house, looked like it had been picked up, twisted around, and then thrown against a tree. It was smashed to pieces. What wasn't destroyed by the wind was left to be drenched by the rain.

Saturday was our second full day at Nemecio's house. My mother felt that even though the winds were still "dangerously strong," we needed some fresh air. She allowed us to creep out through the opening in the wall and see for ourselves the complete desolation that had occurred. We rummaged around in the rubble, the remains of what had been our house, bracing ourselves against the pounding wind while we searched for anything we considered precious or even usable. Although we planted our feet, we could barely keep ourselves upright because of the force of the wind. As careful as we were, making our way through the debris, I managed to step on a nail and screamed out in pain. It was all I could do to hobble back through the opening in the wall.

The winds continued into Saturday night. Although exceedingly grateful, it seemed as though we would never be able to leave the crowded space we had come to call "home" for the last two days. Together, we huddled like hens on the ground, trying to stay warm. (Nemecio did actually own some chickens. When he found them outside and brought them into the house, we noticed the wind had blown off just about all their feathers!)

We were all still wearing the same wet clothes we had arrived in. There's no telling what it smelled like in there! So many people bunched together, the far section of the dirt floor our only bathroom. The days had started to blend together, and each day looked like the last. At night, we slept when we could. It was around midnight on that Saturday night that we noticed an eerie silence. The wind had stopped its incessant wailing. As we sat there in the darkness, we wondered, *Is it over?*

The next morning, Sunday, we continued sorting through the piles of debris, the remains of the contents of our home on full display for all to see. Some elderly people passed by us on their way to church. *Church? What on earth? There is so much to do. Surely, if our house was a pile of rubble, their homes were in similar shape. And was there even a church to go to?* But they had a different outlook. *We are going to church to give thanks to God that not one life was lost.* This is when I learned that God does not need a building for His people to call church. The *church* is the people. Gathered under an old parachute that had been dropped on the island by the US Military with food and other relief items after the devastation caused by typhoon Miding in 1986, the *church* met, praising God for what was most important to them: life!

We heard story after story of God's faithfulness, protection, and answer to their prayers. One family told of how they had run to a neighboring house only to find that they were among seventy-six others who had gathered there to seek refuge. The floor gave way, crashing to the ground, not from the force of the winds but from the weight of the people inside! And yet, they continued to praise God through the storm. We were told that at this house, it was the men's job to save their families by holding the roof in place, and it was the children's responsibility to sing hymns. Others told of how they had fled their homes that were being torn apart by the wind, only to spend the night outside, gripping tree trunks with all their might, praying that their fingers would not be pried apart by the wind.

We had simply lost our possessions. The Ibatan had lost their homes, their fruit trees and gardens, and, most tragically, their rice growing in the fields. And yet, they were praising God. Although my parents had not yet translated the book of Habakkuk, the Ibatan were living out verses 17 and 18 of chapter 3,

> Though the fig tree does not bud and there are no grapes on the vines, though the olive crop fails and the fields produce no food, though there are no sheep in the pen and no cattle in the stalls, yet I will rejoice in the Lord, I will be joyful in God my Savior.[69]

You can choose to believe in fate, in the universe, or in the stars aligning. I chose then and choose to believe now that God is real, and He not only hears our prayers but also answers them. He is the God Who sees, *El Roi*; the God Who provides, *Jireh*; and the God Who loves, *Jesus*. My parents had not yet translated the Old Testament, and yet Isaiah's words rang true for the Ibatan: *"When you pass through the waters, I will be with you; and when you pass through the rivers, they will not sweep over you."*[70]

The rivers themselves had swollen during the storm, and rushing waters had threatened to sweep many away when they had tried to cross the river on their way to safety. The Lord had protected them and watched over them.

Old *Apong* (grandfather) *Gonzalo*, one of the former shamans of the island, had cried out to God in the middle of the storm, *"Father, this house is yours. If you want it, take it. But if not, I could use it for a little longer!"* God heard *Apong Gonzalo's* prayer. Not only was his house untouched by the winds, but the grass on his roof was also not even disturbed! *Apong Gonzalo*, while ancient

---

[69] Habakkuk 3:17–18 (NIV).
[70] Isaiah 43:2 (NIV).

(at least that's how he appeared to me at the time in my childhood, even though he was probably not much past sixty), was young in his Christian walk. And yet his simple, selfless prayer was brimming with faith. It has been almost four decades since *Pepang*, and Apong *Gonzalo* is no longer here on this earth. I believe he is planting heavenly rice fields and offering with joy the best of his harvest to the Lord, his eternal provider. This picture of *Apong Gonzalo* reminds me of Hebrew 12:2: *"Keeping our eyes on Jesus, the champion who initiates and perfects our faith. Because of the joy awaiting him, he endured the cross, disregarding its shame. Now he is seated in the place of honor beside God's throne."*[71] What a hope and a joy we have waiting for us!

By Monday, the winds had died down enough that JAARS could send a pilot with a few basic items for our family. My dad had worked to piece together the antenna so that he could contact the SIL Center at Bagabag and request an emergency flight to Babuyan. My parents made the decision to send my sister and me ahead of them on the return flight, back to our home at the center on the mainland.

As the plane took off from the grass airstrip, I looked down at the devastation below me. The Ibatan classify their typhoons and determine the strength of the winds by the type of trees that are destroyed. A simple tropical depression blows over banana trees and smaller fruit trees. *Miding*, the superstorm that had devastated the island the previous year, had been a coconut tree storm, leveling most of the coconut trees on the island. *Pepang* had been a *narra* tree storm, uprooting huge trees inter-

---

[71] Hebrew 12:2 (NLT)

twined with heavy vines that had taken decades to grow. From high up, the jungle looked as if a giant animal had trampled it. Looking out the window, we watched as our parents grew smaller and smaller. Soon, they disappeared from view, and I could no longer make out the damaged trees on the island.

While *Pepang* remains the strongest typhoon the Ibatan have lived through, it has become a poignant marker in my life. Yes, my family survived the terrifying night flight and lived in a cramped, unfinished house with dirt floors during howling winds and rain for three days. But *Pepang* is not simply a story of survival; it is a story of faith, of courage, of friendship, and of God's miraculous provision. Looking back and reliving memories, I can see the perfect timing of God, the sheltering hand of the Almighty, as He led my family through such a desperate time.

If you ask anyone in our family about the biggest storm we have been through, or even the biggest natural disaster we have been through together, I think we would all probably have the same answer. *Pepang* was a terrifying experience, to say the least. And yet, it is a shared experience that drew us together in a way that no other experience could have done. As a family, we jokingly refer to any type of family event as *"family bonding."* This was family bonding at its height! Not only did we bond together as an immediate family, but we also bonded together with our Ibatan family. God knew that, because of what we had experienced together, our hearts would forever be knit together with the hearts of the Ibatan. From that point on, we were not simply visitors on the island; we were family. To this day, I still refer to those on the island as *maraan* (uncle), *ikit* (auntie), *akang* (older sibling), and *apong* (grandmother/father).

We were told after the devastation of *Pepang*, and even many years later, that the Ibatan saw our discomfort and loss and recognized that, together, we all had lost something. Our fear and our loss were the same as their fear and their loss. Through our fear, we could celebrate together that what we had lost was of such little value compared to what we had been given—life. And in our suffering, we could all truly say together, *"We are hard pressed on every side, but not crushed; perplexed, but not in despair; persecuted, but not abandoned; struck down, but not destroyed."*[72]

I often wonder how our relationship with the Ibatan would have turned out had we not been on the island that week in October. If we had been on the mainland, far from the destructive force of the winds and rain that came that week, would the Ibatan have truly accepted us as a family? Would my parents have had as much help and support from the Ibatan to complete the translation of the New Testament in the time frame that they did? Would we have come to love and appreciate the Ibatan as much as we do now if we had not endured *Pepang* together? As a seven-year-old, these thoughts were obviously not something I concerned myself with; however, so many years later, I find myself marveling at God's timing.

There is an obvious comparison that can be made between weathering life's storms and *Pepang*, the storm my family endured. Emotional storms can be devastating and debilitating, and I don't want to discount the pain

---

[72] 2 Corinthians 4:8–9 (NIV).

and turmoil of these storms. I have been through many myself that I will refer to in another chapter, but there is something to be said about experiencing an actual, physical threat to your life. Living through a traumatic, life-threatening experience has a way of drawing you to the Father, the Creator of life. I stand in awe at the miraculous wonder of what happened in those few days—those days that seemed like an eternity. Not one life was lost. Apostle Paul encourages those with him during a terrible storm at sea, *"But take courage! None of you will lose your lives, even though the ship will go down."*[73] While most of the Ibatan lost their homes, their fields, and even their fishing boats, no one lost their lives.

Surviving is more than just enduring. It is the steadfast perseverance through the trial. It is how we come out on the other side and how we live to tell the story of our struggles, praising God that He turns them into triumphs, all for His glory.

---

[73] Acts 27:22 (NLT).

Eight

~~Failure~~ Restoration

Restore to me the joy of your salvation and grant me a willing spirit, to sustain me.

Psalm 51:12

Every little girl dreams of her wedding day. The dress, the flowers, the cake, the groom. As a child, I imagined that my wedding day would be perfect. Like many little girls, I dreamed that, on my wedding day, I would somehow be transformed into royalty with a beautiful dress. Princess for a day, I would be whisked away by my prince charming to live a magical life with very few problems and would live to tell my great-grandchildren wonderful tales of our adventures together, sort of like Buttercup in *The Princess Bride*. She was rescued by William, and they literally rode off into the sunset on a white horse to live a perfect *mawwage* filled with love and laughter.[74]

Obviously, this is a fairy tale and not exactly what happened to me (and most likely didn't happen to you

---

[74] *The Princess Bride*, directed by Rob Reiner (20th Century Fox, 1987).

either). I suppose that I would be doing not only myself but also anyone who might read this book a disservice if I left out the messy part of my life. *Failure.* It's a big word, one that many people, particularly me, are often afraid of. Of course, none of us want to fail. None of us choose to fail, and we certainly don't like to admit we failed. But failure happens, and we have a choice: face our failures head-on or cower behind them in self-pity. And so, I purposely left the word *failure* in the title of this chapter. And I purposely crossed it out because God is in the business of restoration. We can choose to enlarge our failures, hiding behind them in misery, or accept the goodness of God's healing and, in doing so, become completely restored.

At the age of twenty, I married a friend with whom I had attended high school at Faith Academy. While I'm sure at the beginning we both had every intention of growing old together, our marriage lasted a grand total of three years. In truth, there were problems in our relationship, one of which was that our marriage became rather crowded quite early on. Many signs pointed to his infidelity, but as a young bride, I was afraid to acknowledge them. Because if I acknowledged the signs, I would have to believe that they occurred and that would make the affair true.

Looking back, I can see that I was in a state of paralysis, unable to make a move, frozen in fear and defeat. I don't really know how long the affair lasted or how many affairs there were. That is not the focus or intent of this book. What I do know is that my heart must answer to the Lord, and that every person must make a decision to be obedient to Christ. While I am certainly affected by the actions of others and subsequently the consequences of those decisions, I am not responsible for those choices. And in that, there is freedom.

My intention in discussing my failed marriage is not to condemn my ex-husband or anyone else who may have gone through a divorce. Neither is it to condone separation or divorce. (In fact, I firmly believe in the sanctity of marriage originally outlined in scripture as that of one man and one woman for the duration of their natural lives.[75]) The purpose of sharing about my failed marriage is not to tell of the pain and heartache I experienced or to air my dirty laundry. My intent is to declare God's faithfulness, His goodness, His kindness, His compassion, and His love for me especially during this difficult time in my life. It is to proclaim victory over sin and sorrow.

Restoration happened in a completely different way for me than I had prayed for. My marriage was not restored, but I certainly was. It was an inward restoration where God redeemed my grief for His glory and turned my anguish into joy.[76] God showed me many things about my frailty and also about His steadfast faithfulness.

During those times when I felt rejected, living out my life as a statistic, I was reminded that I was never abandoned, never alone, and never discarded by the Lord. Matthew says that those who seek will find.[77] I certainly found God in a deeply personal way in the midst of my sorrow, and because of that, I can say that I am changed. *"But may all who seek you rejoice and be glad in*

---

[75] Matthew 19:4–6, Mark 10:6–9.
[76] Isaiah 61:3.
[77] Matthew 7:7–8 (NIV).

you; may those who love your salvation always say, 'Let God be exalted!'"[78]

Although you already know the outcome of my story, I believe quite firmly that God is in the business of reconciliation and that, in His mighty power, He can and does reunite and restore broken marriages. Saving a marriage is not hard for God. It is hard for us as humans. Anyone who has been married for any length of time knows that marriage takes work, lots of it. While God always answers prayers, He simultaneously allows us to make our own choices. Sometimes the choices of others make it extremely difficult to move toward restoration. And this is where I found myself.

Ephesians 4:32 says, *"Be kind and compassionate to one another, forgiving each other, just as in Christ God forgave you."*[79] If husbands and wives could truly act in kindness toward each other, forgiving small grievances before they become hurdles too big to jump over, how many more marriages might be saved from the pain and sorrow of divorce? A picture of God's steadfast and enduring love for His bride, the church, is His desire for all marriages to thrive and grow.

Sometimes it can be hard to be kind and compassionate to a harsh spouse. It is hard to forgive when there is pain and injustice. But in Ephesians, the apostle Paul doesn't give us stipulations for when or how to forgive. He simply says to forgive. If Christ can forgive our sins, replacing our condemnation with redemption, can we not take the step to at least move toward forgiveness for those in our lives who have wronged us? We certainly

---

[78] Psalm 70:4 (NIV).
[79] Ephesians 4:32 (NIV).

cannot control the actions of others, but we can choose our response to situations that seem out of our control. Our decision to forgive can directly impact the rest of our lives. Regardless of whether the person who wronged us apologizes or not, the decision to forgive is a choice to ask for God's grace to permeate our hearts, rather than allow bitterness and resentment to fester, eating away at us until hatred takes root.

The Bible is very clear when it comes to marriage. One man. One woman. For life.

> "For I hate divorce!" says the Lord, the God of Israel. "To divorce your wife is to overwhelm her with cruelty," says the Lord of Heaven's Armies. "So guard your heart; do not be unfaithful to your wife."[80]

To divorce your wife during the time this was written would mean that the woman would not be taken care of and would not be able to remarry. She would remain alone, an outcast, not even considered a widow, so that others could care for her, and thus, it would be a "cruel" act to place her in a position of abandonment. While our society today provides a myriad of work opportunities for women of all economic and social statuses, the concept of casting someone aside remains the same. Divorce conveys a selfish disregard for the other person, leading to feelings of being discarded. The obvious hurt from rejection leaves deep wounds that often take years (and possibly counseling) before healing can take place. The

---

[80] Malachi 2:16 (NLT).

decision to divorce a spouse is a choice to disentangle, tear oneself away from, or be apart from the other. The two that became one are now being ripped apart. While it has become fairly easy these days to cast a spouse aside in divorce, what cannot be separated from this event are the multitude of far-reaching consequences that result from divorce.

While it is clear what the Bible says about the sanctity and longevity of marriage, please hear me when I say that I am not advocating for a spouse to stay in a violent or unsafe circumstance for them or any children who might be present. While I did experience some physical circumstances that were violent in nature (which I praise God that I was able to remove myself from), this is not the focus of my story. If you are in an abusive situation, please seek help from family, friends, church leaders, and counselors. There are many wonderful Christian counselors who can walk you through the practical steps you might need to take for your own safety and that of any children who might be in the home.

I believe that I tried everything I could to move toward reconciliation because of my firm conviction that marriage is sacred. I pleaded with the Lord to move mountains, restore my marriage, and change the heart of my spouse so that we could be reunited. I sought godly counsel from my parents, spiritual mentors, and church leaders. I sought out a Christian counselor (even when at the time it seemed as though my budget would not be able to accommodate the fees) and prayed earnestly for direction, wisdom, and, ultimately, reconciliation.

What I discovered through many months of heartache, however, is that no matter how many steps toward reconciliation and healing I took, I could not force my spouse to take those same steps. I was not responsible for his choices. I was only accountable for the decisions I made. Once again, I found myself in between worlds, waffling between anger and self-pity, and choosing to allow the Holy Spirit to pierce my heart with the truth from God's Word so that healing and restoration could happen, regardless of what the outcome of my marriage ended up being.

As a Canadian married to a Canadian living in Canada, a year of separation is required before a legal divorce can be granted by the courts (or at least it was at the time of my divorce). To some, this may seem like a punishment. To others, it might feel like an opportunity—extra time to try and manipulate the other person into staying married. Looking back, I believe this year of separation was a gift from God for me. It was a time to discover my true identity as a child of God, not as "Mrs. So and So," but as my names suggest—beautiful and precious in God's eyes. I'm not going to lie and say that it was an easy time. For the most part, I felt like I was in limbo, floating between worlds. I was twenty-three years old, out of college, and living on my own, but I wasn't technically single. I still had my ex-husband's last name and signed any papers, documents, and even letters to parents that I sent home with my students with that last name. Since I was a fairly new bride, my identity had been wrapped up in my new title as "Mrs.," and my piano students still used this prefix. So for a year, I waffled back and forth between going back to my maiden name of Maree and just keeping my married last name to avoid the hassle.

During that year of separation, I poured over my Bible daily, underlining any verse that offered hope with a red pen, or that showed God's love for the brokenhearted. I remember longing for the stillness at night at the end of a long day when I could crawl under the covers, turn on my lamp, and read God's Word. I had the expectation that every time I opened my Bible, God would speak to me and lead me to verses that provided comfort, healing, and direction. I was never disappointed, but I certainly had some nagging questions. What was I to do if, after a year, I hadn't heard from my husband? What would I do if, after a year, he refused to reconcile? I felt like David who cried out to God, *"Even my close friend, whom I trusted, he who shared my bread, has lifted up his heel against me."*[81] Would I forever be trapped in limbo, married to a ghost, someone I would never even see, who was in a relationship with someone else? I knew that God hated divorce. I knew that this was not God's plan for our marriage. And yet, I felt trapped and exhausted under the weight of the unknown. I didn't know what to do.

Our early attempts at couples' marital counseling had been unsuccessful. Sitting on the couch during our sessions, I felt stuck. Whenever I felt even a small amount of progress had been made, we would encounter a setback.

Before we were separated, I found a phone bill in the trash. In the long list of numbers called, there was a number I recognized, her number. It appeared multiple times. This was after the promise had been made to cut ties and stop all communication with her. I was crushed. Would there ever be an end to their affair? Would it ever just be the two of us in our marriage? Could I return to a marriage where trust was nonexistent? I wrestled with

---

[81] Psalm 41:9 (NIV).

these thoughts over and over again for the year we lived apart. Crying out to the Lord in the darkness and searching the Scriptures for answers were part of my daily routine. "*O Lord, you have seen this; be not silent. Do not be far from me, O Lord.*"[82] What would the rest of my life look like?

During this time, I was working three jobs and preparing to take my ARCT Piano Performance exam (Associate of the Royal Conservatory of Music, Toronto, Canada). A typical day would begin in the darkness of the early morning. I would flick on the lamp by my bed, read a Psalm, make some coffee, and head to the piano, trying to get at least forty-five minutes to an hour of practice before heading to the office for an 8:00 a.m. start to my workday.

During my time as a student at Trinity Western University, I worked a secretarial job and later served as the admissions coordinator for the Canada Institute of Linguistics (CanIL). By two in the afternoon, I was racing home from the linguistics office, trying to give myself a few minutes to use the restroom, make some tea, and be ready for my first piano student to walk in the door at three. By the time nine rolled around, I was exhausted and hungry. After a quick dinner, I would be back at the piano, practicing until eleven, sometimes even after midnight. On the weekends, I worked at the local music store, selling music books. Of course, this type of lifestyle was not sustainable, and I often found myself sick. I remember underlining a particular passage in my Bible, "*Be merciful to me, O Lord, for I am in distress; my eyes grow week with sorrow, my soul and my body with grief. My*

---

[82] Psalm 35:22 (NIV).

life is consumed by anguish and my years by groaning; my strength fails because of my affliction, and my bones grow weak."[83]

By the time the year was up, I had read through not only the Psalms but also the prophets multiple times. I don't think there is a Psalm in my Bible that is not marked up by pen; passages underlined, circled, and dated; and margins filled with questions, insights, and answers to prayer. What is not visible to the human eye are the tearstains. Those tears revealed not only the immense sorrow that welled up from inside my soul but also the flood of joy and hope, knowing that my worth and identity are found solely in Christ. His grace for me superseded my pain, my grief, and my feelings of incompleteness, unworthiness, doubt, and fear. I discovered in the darkness that I was never abandoned. Never alone. God's faithfulness to me has never been so evident as during that year of separation. In my loneliness, the Lord was a listening ear; in my weakness, He was my rock that I was assured would hold me up; in my desperation, He was my hope. Richard Foster states this so eloquently.

> Through all of this, paradoxically, God is purifying our faith by threatening to destroy it. We are led to a profound and holy distrust of all superficial drives and human strivings. We know more deeply than ever before our capacity for infinite self-deception. Slowly we are being taken off of vain securities and false

---

[83] Psalm 31:9–10 (NIV).

> allegiances. Our trust in all exterior and interior results is being shattered so that we can learn faith in God alone. Through our barrenness of soul God is producing detachment, humility, patience and perseverance.[84]

It was never my desire or intention to be the one to file for divorce. My decision to file for divorce did not come lightly. I had prayed diligently during the year of separation for two things: grace and courage. Grace to forgive, to not allow bitterness to fester in my heart, and courage to move forward no matter what road lay ahead of me, knowing that I was not alone.

While I was not the one who had committed adultery, I knew that I would be held responsible for my actions and my response to my unexpected life circumstances. I would be asked to account for every careless word, every wayward thought, and every unkind action. I prayed for forgiveness, for wisdom, for peace, and for discernment. While I bear the scars of a failed marriage, I also bear witness to the redemptive, healing work of Christ in my life.

During this time, I read Psalm 31 over and over, clinging to what I knew to be true about God's character.

> But I trust in you, O Lord; I say, "You are my God." My times are in your hands; deliver me from my enemies and from those who pursue me. Let your face shine on your servant;

---
[84] Richard J. Foster, *Prayer*, 22.

> save me in your unfailing love. Let
> me not be put to shame, O Lord, for
> I have cried out to you.[85]

I believe the Lord answered my prayers, giving me the courage not only to show grace and forgive my ex-husband but also to accept my loss, claim victory for my life, and dare to have a vision for my future.

On one particularly difficult night, I remember tossing and turning, desperate for the reprieve of sleep. Apparently, I finally went to sleep because I woke up the next morning with a dream still fresh in my mind—a dream so real that I can almost think back on it as an actual memory. In my dream, I had been flipping through a photo album. The dream was hazy, and the people around me were blurry, but the pictures in the photo album were clear. There were pictures of me and small children, who I instantly knew belonged to me, celebrating a birthday party. That was it. That was the whole dream. But it was enough for me to know that God cared about me, about the deepest desires of my heart. I believe He gave me that dream as something to hold on to, a picture of hope.

God is not in the business of destroying dreams, but of building them. As I was reading my Bible one day, I came across a passage in the book of Joel: *"I will repay you for the years the locusts have eaten...you will have plenty to eat, until you are full, and you will praise the name of the Lord your God who has worked wonders for you."*[86] Over the years, I have clung to these verses, knowing that the

---

[85] Psalm 31:14–17a (NIV).
[86] Joel 2:25a–26 (NLT).

years in my life that were devastated by locusts—where I felt picked clean, withered, and dry, with nothing left to give—were not in vain.

There is another very well-known Bible verse in the book of Jeremiah that says *"for I know the plans I have for you', declares the Lord, 'plans to prosper you and not to harm you, plans to give you a hope and a future."*[87] This verse is often used at graduations, giving hope and vision to young students as they embark on their future endeavors. While I wasn't on the cusp of graduation, I took this verse to heart, knowing that even if my future was unclear to me, even if it meant staying married to a man I could not trust, or even if it meant being alone, I could trust that God would keep His promise and would never leave me. HE would be my future. I was *"learning the obedience of settled peace in the expectation of events beyond [my] control."* If we know that we can trust God and His character, we can then *"crawl into the Father's lap and receive his love and comfort and healing and strength… and we can worship deep within our spirit."*[88]

The divorce was finalized three months after I filed. It was not contested. I found myself newly single at the age of twenty-four, feeling as though I had already lived a lifetime. While at peace with my decision, I was unsure of my new role as a newly divorced single. But being single again really had no bearing on my social life. I had no time for extracurriculars.

When I wasn't at work, I was practicing piano. Somehow, I knew that I wasn't ready to take the ARCT Piano Performer's exam, but I had to try. I had spent more

---

[87] Jeremiah 29:11 (NIV).
[88] Richard J. Foster, *Prayer*, 72, 135.

than I had financially for lessons twice a week as well as paying for all my theory prerequisite exams, not to mention the countless hours spent practicing. I prayed once again for the courage to play my unpolished pieces and the grace to forgive myself for the inevitable outcome.

The day of my exam came. I knew in my gut as soon as I had finished that there was no hope of me passing. My trills in the Mozart Sonata were sloppy at best, I had several memory fluctuations in the Bach, and my tempo was shaky throughout both the Rachmaninoff and the Liszt. (What was I thinking preparing both a Rachmaninoff and a Liszt anyway? Could I not have picked at least one piece that was a little less intense?) Several weeks later, my results were in. I had failed.

Even though I had prepared myself in advance for this outcome, seeing my final mark was a blow that was hard to take. Now I had another choice to make. Would I let this failure define me as a musician, as a teacher, and as an individual? Or would I take what I had learned and strive to do better the next time around, perhaps when I was more emotionally stable! Once again, I prayed for grace to accept my failure and the courage to take hold of the promises God laid out for me in Scripture. *"'Restrain your voice from weeping and your eyes from tears, for your work will be rewarded,' declares the Lord."*[89] I knew I couldn't spend the rest of my life withering because of failure, and so I chose to embrace what was to come and claim that *"there is hope for your future,' declares the Lord."*[90] I chose to view this failure as a temporary setback, one that I refused to let define me. God had proven

---

[89] Jeremiah 31:16a (NIV).
[90] Jeremiah 31:17 (NIV).

Himself faithful to me throughout my year of separation and divorce, and I knew that I could once again trust Him to guide me through the deep sense of inadequacy and rejection that I found myself once again tempted to hide behind. I was reminded that the Lord invited me to take refuge in Him *"in the shadow of [His] wings until the disaster has passed."*[91]

I am thankful that during this time, the Lord provided friendships for me that I still value and treasure to this day. Without their constant love for me, I know I would have succumbed to much darker thoughts. The Lord is truly faithful, full of love and compassion, and He knew exactly what I needed at that time to help draw me out of the depths of the sorrow and despair I felt. *"Oh Lord my God, I called to you for help, and you healed me. O Lord, you brought me up from the grave."*[92]

Marlaena ("LP," or "Life Partner" as we called each other) is truly my friend for life. She is a remarkable lady whom my children call "Auntie" and who is deserving of her own chapter in this book. She is without a doubt the most steadfast and loyal friend I could ever have asked for.

Chuck and Patty MacKnee sacrificed much for me. We attended the same church, and although they were nearer to my parents' age, I became friends with not only their adult children (who were about my age) but also with them. I had served on the same worship team as Chuck and his son and had also traveled with Chuck on a mission trip, along with other individuals from our

---

[91] Psalm 57:1 (NIV).
[92] Psalm 30:2–3 (NIV).

church, to Mexico to build two houses for families in dire need of a home.

During this difficult time in my life when I felt stranded, caught in between worlds, they not only took time (literally hours and days) out of their busy schedules to comfort me, feed me, and take care of me, but they also prayed with me and for me. In essence, they absorbed me into their family. I will never forget the night I called Patty and said, *"I'm scared. I'm coming over!"* She had a bed ready for me, arms open to hug me, and a heart ready to listen. I am forever grateful for their friendship, sound advice, mentorship, endless coffee, walks along the Fort-to-Fort Trail, and genuine concern for my well-being.

Other church friends rallied around me as well, supported me with hugs, laughter, and most importantly, prayer. Maia, a bright ray of sunshine to my soul, and Bill and Carey, who opened their home to me in more than one country, are among the dear friends who not only sustained me but also uplifted me. Corrie, whom I affectionately referred to as "VanTol," and Natasha, lovingly called "Natty," even subjected themselves to five days in a cramped two-door civic, as they accompanied me to my new home in Texas. That is what you call true friendship! All of these individuals mentioned were loyal friends I had met at church, had a deep love for the Lord, and who brightened my day with their encouragement and care for me.

Richard Foster states that *"while the wilderness is necessary, it is never meant to be permanent. In God's time and in God's way the desert will give way to a land flowing with milk and honey."* So in the desert, our job is to trust that an oasis of milk and honey will indeed one day be a reality. *"He invites us to see and to hear what is around us and, through it all, to discern the footprints of the Holy.*" If our eyes are blinded by bitterness, if our ears are deaf to praise, then we are missing the blessings of milk and honey before us. We see them simply as a mirage and not an oasis. As we trust Him,

> the suffering is not for nothing! God takes it and uses it for something beautiful, something far beyond anything we can imagine. Right now we catch only glimpses here and there, the moon's reflected light. But a day is coming when the blinders will be removed and the scales will fall off, and then we will see a glory in our sufferings that will blaze like the noonday sun.[93]

Friend, if you find yourself in what seems like an impossible situation, please hear me when I say that the Lord sees you. I do not pretend to know or understand your suffering, but I know of One Who does. His suffering was so great that He died on the cross. He endured all things so that you and I might have life.

"*I, even I am the Lord, and apart from me there is no savior. I have revealed and saved and proclaimed…yes, and from ancient days I am he.*"[94] When you feel blinded by sorrow, cling to His promise that says, "*I will lead the blind by ways they have not known, along unfamiliar paths I will guide them; I will turn the darkness into light before*

---

[93] Richard J. Foster, *Prayer*, 24, 28, 220.
[94] Isaiah 43:11–12 (NLT).

them and make the rough places smooth. These are the things I will do; I will not forsake them."[95] When you are afraid, when you feel paralyzed by what might lie ahead, know that He calls you by name and will guide you as you choose to trust Him.

> Fear not, for I have redeemed you; I have summoned you by name; you are mine. When you pass through the waters I will be with you; and when you pass through the rivers, they will not sweep over you. When you walk through the fire you will not be burned.[96]

Claim His promises for yourself, acknowledge your failures, and cling to the promise of the blessings and hope for a future that is far beyond what we can even make up in our wildest dreams. Dare to believe that He holds your future. "*See, I am doing a new thing! Now it springs up; do you not perceive it?*"[97]

---

[95] Isaiah 42:16 (NIV).
[96] Isaiah 43:1b–2a (NIV).
[97] Isaiah 43:19 (NIV).

Nine

Family Conflab

*Because he has turned his ear to me,
I will call on him as long as I live.*

Psalm 116:2

My dear dad always has a way to remember things. A song to learn the names of the twelve disciples, another song for the books of the Bible, or some type of alliteration for the main points of every sermon he gave. It was no different when it came to figuring out how to handle life's major decisions. "*The Three Ds,*" as he called them, or "*Dad's Three Ds,*" as I like to refer to them, was a valuable legacy that my grandpa Maree passed down to my father. He, in turn, has passed this saying down to both me and my sister, and it has helped me wade through the pros and cons of every significant decision I have had to make in my adolescent and adult years.

If I was more clever, I might be able to come up with a creative *D* word to replace the word *three* in the title, like dynamic or distinguished, or something along those lines, but to me, that makes it too complicated.

"Dad's three *D*s" has served me well, and although simplistic in its name, its message is profound.

Growing up, decision-making was taken seriously in our house, and my parents were very willing to include my sister and me in the discussion process. We often called these times "family conflab." I'm not sure where that name originated, who thought of it first, or why we agreed to call our family discussions by such a strange name, but somehow, it stuck.

Occasionally, when my mom or dad would call us into the living room and say, "Time for family conflab!" I knew that new information was going to be discussed. I remember the time that we had a "family conflab" over whether we wanted to go to Faith Academy for high school. My parents laid out all the options: go to the local public Filipino school, have our mom homeschool us, or attend boarding school at Faith Academy, located about ten hours away in the capital city of Manila. While this, I'm sure, was a very serious and difficult decision for my parents, my sister and I were unanimous in our decision to attend boarding school. Family conflab over!

Other family conflab discussions weren't always as life defining as which high school I should attend. Other times, we unofficially began family conflabs during our evening family devotions after dinner. Our natural conversations led to family decisions about what to have for dinner the next day, who would go to the public market with mom in the morning, where we would be allowed to have a sleepover with friends, or how many green mangos were too many to eat in one sitting. Our family was used to discussing issues both big and small together. Looking back, family conflab, whether an official call to order or a casual discussion around the table, bonded our family together in a unique way.

Family conflab created an atmosphere in our home that was centered around conversation. This overflowed into our adolescent and adult years. I can recall many times when I picked up the phone to call my mom and dad for a type of informal family conflab session. I have also sat for hours in my dad's basement office to sort through a topic I was arguing about in a college paper or to sift through the pros and cons of a major life crossroads I was approaching. My parents were always willing to listen (and still are), and I knew I could count on them for an honest, practical approach to a decision. The first thing they always asked me was, "Have you prayed about it?" I found their counsel to be not only wise but also a tremendous example of forming the deeply entrenched spiritual habit of talking to God.

And so, it is perhaps not surprising that the first *D* in "Dad's three *D*s" is *discuss*. "Who have you discussed this issue with?" my dad would ask. "Have you discussed it with the Lord? Have you discussed it with your friends? Have you discussed it with spiritual mentors?" These questions would prompt me to, first, get on my knees and ask the Lord for wisdom and then evaluate which of my friends I trusted most deeply with the decisions with which I had been wrestling. Which friends would not only listen with their hearts but would also offer practical and spiritual wisdom. Who did I consider spiritually mature in my life? Who would stand with me and intercede before God to help me navigate the uncertainty of what I was experiencing?

In previous chapters, I have noted significant people in my life who have stood by me, often at the expense of their own time and resources, and who have offered their friendship at no cost to me. These individuals I treasure deeply. Thank you to those friends who offered up wisdom, even if it was not what I wanted to hear at the time.

As I look back on the decisions I have had to make in my life, I realize that I was never alone in those decisions. While not all my decisions were easy (and even after I had made a decision, some still felt uncertain), I can honestly say that I have yet to make a major life decision blindly. I'm certainly not saying that all the decisions I made were the correct ones, but one way or another, I made a calculated choice.

I believe that God honors our desire to seek Him, that He does not laugh at our mistakes, and that He can take our frail, human attempts at discernment and use them to teach us and fashion us to be more like Himself. Brennan Manning says regarding the decision-making process, *"It is trusting enough in Jesus to make mistakes and believing enough that His life will still pulse within us."* Sometimes the decision might meet with the disapproval of those we are close to. But as Manning says, we must have *"a courageous determination to make unpopular decisions that are expressive of the truth of who we are—not of who we think we should be or who someone else wants us to be."*[98] Knowing that we are children of God and, if we are in truth, seeking the Lord with a pure heart, we can rest knowing that we are expressing the truth of who we are as children of God and what we believe God is calling us to do.

---

[98] Brennan Manning, *The Rabbi's Heartbeat* (Colorado Springs: NavPress, 2003), 103.

In January 2006, I was presented with the opportunity to join a team of individuals on a short mission trip to Cambodia. This team was comprised of individuals from various parts of the United States who had set aside eleven days to serve the children at the orphanage and nutrition centers that MANNA Worldwide had established in Phnom Penh, Cambodia, and the surrounding areas. MANNA Worldwide is a nonprofit Christian organization that partners with missionaries to *"rescue children from the grip of poverty."* Their purpose is to blend practical and impactful community development initiatives, such as access to clean water, nutrition centers, schools, medical facilities, and orphanages with the life-changing power of the Gospel. I had no idea that when I signed up to join this mission team, I would be the one presented with a life-altering decision.

As the only Canadian in the group, I joined the rest of the team in Phnom Penh from Vancouver. I knew only one other person who would be on the trip: a friend and classmate from high school at Faith Academy. While attending our seventh (yes, seventh, not tenth!) high school reunion, I had spoken with Keith about my recent acceptance to grad school but was unsure of whether that was really the direction I wanted to pursue.

Not long before this trip to Cambodia, Keith had joined MANNA Worldwide's staff and invited me to meet him and the rest of the team in Cambodia. His father, Bruce, is the founder of MANNA Worldwide and at the time was the CEO and president. I vaguely remembered Bruce and his wife, Pam, from my days in the Philippines, only having met them one or two times at a volleyball game or around the time of my high school graduation. I was beyond excited to once again be going to Asia but had no idea that, by the end of the trip, Bruce and fellow director, Chuck Ward, would offer me a position at the MANNA Worldwide headquarters in Fort Worth, Texas.

One day, during our time in Cambodia, our team visited the Stueng Mean Chey landfill. Growing up in Asia, I had certainly been exposed to poverty: the squatters that riddled the banks of the Pasig River in Manila, the rows of cardboard and tin shacks stacked side by side in Escopa, alleyways lined with garbage, and the backbreaking efforts of those planting rice in flooded, muddy fields up to their knees. These are images that are seared into my memory. But the Stueng Mean Chey landfill, for some reason, made me weep.

Amid the trash heap was a little girl. A doll's head kept her company. I'm not exactly sure why I wept that day. Perhaps I felt that even in my desperation, loneliness, and abandonment, I had never been truly alone. I had my Heavenly Father to comfort and carry me. This child had no one. I wanted to rescue her from the dump, from the refuse of her miserable life. Isn't it true that that's what our Heavenly Father does for us? He rescues us, washes us clean from the filth of our sin, and cradles us close to Him, clean, whole, and pure?

In 1 Samuel, it says, "*He raises the poor from the dust and lifts the needy from the ash heap; he seats them with princes and has them inherit a throne of honor.*"[99] If this is what the Lord did for me in my desperation and failure, how much more would He do for such a small child? And yet how would that child ever know the saving grace of Jesus unless someone showed her Who Jesus was? I can

---

[99] 1 Samuel 2:8 (NIV).

still see that little girl today, and my heart longs to see her again one day in heaven, smiling and dancing, with one hand holding a doll, the other hand holding fast to the hand of her Father in heaven.

Ten days later, after our time in Cambodia was over, I made the long flight back to Vancouver, Canada. I had a hundred questions running through my mind. What on earth had just happened? I had spent over a week playing with the children at the orphanage and nutrition centers, serving food, passing out toys, and truly embracing not only the children around me but also the pull on my heart for missions. I had felt my soul come alive. The heaviness from the years leading up to my separation and divorce had left me weary, struggling to keep my head out of the fog. For the first time in a long time, I felt like I could see clearly.

It's amazing what happens when you lay aside your own sorrows and start to serve others. When I look back at the pictures that I took with the children from that trip, I see genuine smiles, both on the faces of the children and on mine—an overflow of a truly joyful heart. I knew then that, somehow, mission work would be part of my future.

Even though I was able to acknowledge the tug on my heart to be involved in mission work after that trip, there were still some practical questions I needed answers to. What was I to do? Taking the job with MANNA Worldwide would mean moving from Canada to Texas. Of all the states in the United States, I perhaps dreaded Texas the most. I'm not exactly sure why, as I had no memories of my time in Texas as a one-year-old, but perhaps my ideas of Texas were partly shaped by my parent's experiences of living in Texas in the early 1980s. My parents had lived in Cedar Hill while my dad attended graduate school at the University of Texas in Arlington to complete his second master's degree. My dad was a full-time student, while my mom managed to maintain the home, take care of my sister and me, and help my dad type up his school papers. My parents' stories of their time in Texas did not reflect the most treasured moments of their lives! Other than that, my impressions of Texas included images of the wild west, cowboys, cacti, and a type of English that I was guaranteed not to understand (and was it even English?).

I had also just been accepted to graduate school at Trinity Western University and was due to start classes in a few months. My piano teaching business was taking off, and I had started to become more involved in my church, playing on the worship team and helping to facilitate a small group table discussion each week with Alpha (a ministry designed to teach the basic concepts of what it means to be a Christ follower to new Christians and those searching for answers to life's biggest questions). I had even joined a small group. Was the Lord opening an opportunity for me that would mean giving all this up? What would it take for me to move to Texas? Could I leave my church, my friends, and my family behind and start over?

On that long plane ride home from Cambodia, I started to think about who I would need to discuss this new opportunity with. I knew that if I was serious about considering this position, I would also need to get busy praying.

My parents, who, at the time, were still living in Asia and had been dividing their time between the Philippines and Cambodia, where they served as the lead translation consultants for several New Testament translations, listened with open hearts. As expected, they invited me to earnestly pray and ask God to show me clearly if this job was something I should pursue. My mother especially prayed that if this was not God's will, I would see obvious signs that this was not the direction I should go and that the door to this new opportunity would be firmly shut.

I recalled her banana prayers and knew that, this time, she would pray for a downpour instead of sprinkling rain! As I looked back through my Bible, I noticed that a few months before my trip to Cambodia, I had once again been reading through the Psalms. Next to one passage, I noted in the margin, *"Future plans/direction."* As I reread Psalm 143, I realized that the Lord had been directing my steps all along. He had led me to attend my seventh high school reunion, had allowed me the opportunity to speak with Keith, and had given me the boldness to venture out on my own to Cambodia. *"Cause me to hear Your lovingkindness in the morning, for in You do I trust; cause me to know the way in which I should walk, for I lift up my soul to You."*[100] I began to feel more and more at peace with the idea of moving to Texas to join MANNA Worldwide, knowing that if God was opening up a path for me, I could step out in confidence, knowing that He would sustain me.

And yet, I had a long road ahead of me if I was going to join MANNA Worldwide. I still had not told my closest friends. I wondered what their reaction would be when I told them I was considering not only a career move but also an international move to the United States. As I began to share what I had experienced in Cambodia

---

[100] Psalm 143:8 (NIV).

with the rest of my family and friends, my excitement began to grow. My friends provided sound advice without any negative feedback, especially Marlaena. We had become instant friends the first time we met that day long ago, selling music books at a local music store. God knew that we would need each other in the coming months and years after that first meeting.

Marlaena and I had walked the same sorrowful road of separation and divorce at the same time. I can remember one particularly difficult night when I had called Marlaena to come help me move my belongings out of the home I had shared with my husband. Because I didn't have any suitcases, she calmly and quickly, without any questions, grabbed some garbage bags and began filling them with my things. I spent several months living in her guest bedroom after that night and realized then that I had a true and deep *bosom buddy*, a true and forever-lasting best friend. I believe even Anne of Green Gables would have been jealous of our friendship! Over baked Lay's potato chips and a glass of wine, Marlaena and I would joke that there was truly nothing that we could hide from each other.

The process of deciding to move to Texas was no different. While I know that it was difficult for Marlaena to hear me tell her of my possible move, I knew from the moment I spilled my guts to her that she understood the longing in my heart for something more than the grief-ridden life we had both been living. I remember her telling me that she could see in my face and the way I described my experience in Cambodia that peace had settled in my heart. For as long as I have known Marlaena, I have admired her fierce determination to make the most out of life. Her tenacity continues to this day as she not only spent seven years living and working in Australia, but she also opened and has sustained a successful music school that enrolls hundreds of students each year. She is now remarried to a wonderful, Christian gentleman who treats her with the utmost love and respect. Her love for the Lord, her faith and vision for a joyful future, and her determination to pursue life instead of tallying up the heartaches she has experienced are remarkable. It was no surprise to me that Marlaena challenged me to dream of a life beyond the borders of sorrow and grief.

I am so grateful to my friends and family for their patience with me as I mulled over the decision to move to Texas and join MANNA Worldwide. I'm sure that because this weighed so heavily on my mind, it must have dominated every conversation we had! Truthfully, I am thankful for solid, supportive friends who dared to ask me, "*Where are you at in the decision-making process?*" and who lovingly challenged me to pray boldly for answers.

Matthew 7:7–8 says, "*Ask and it will be given to you; seek and you will find; knock and the door will be opened to you. For everyone who asks receives; he who seeks finds; and to him who knocks, the door will be opened.*"[101] I believe the Lord honors the honest and simple prayers of His children because He cares for us and loves us. "*He does not forget the cry of the humble.*"[102] And because we know He sees and hears us, we can trust His word and know that He will be faithful to us. No matter what the outcome is of whatever decisions we are faced with, we can rely on His sovereignty, and as King David did, we can

---

[101] Matthew 7:7–8 (NIV).
[102] Psalm 9:12b (NIV).

also declare, *"I will praise you, O Lord, with my whole heart."*[103]

At times, while it might seem that we are stabbing in the dark, unsure of which path to take, we don't need to live in fear of making a decision blindly. God's promises hold true. *"For I, the Lord your God, will hold your right hand, saying to you, 'Fear not, I will help you.'"*[104]

Therefore, we can say with confidence, *"I will look to the Lord; I will wait for the God of my salvation; My God will hear me."*[105]

---

[103] Psalm 9:1a (NIV).
[104] Isaiah 41:13 (NIV).
[105] Micah 7:7 (NIV).

Ten

The Great Belladonna Took

*For the Lord gives wisdom; from his mouth
come knowledge and understanding.*

Proverbs 2:6

Decision-making is difficult and often tedious, particularly when you spend a good majority of the process discussing options with others. For progress to be made, however, the decision itself requires action. All the discussion in the world isn't going to move you any further down the decision-making process if you don't decide to do something. At some point, the discourse has to stop, and a decision must be made, otherwise, it's just talk.

Taking a step in any direction is always the hardest part, however, because deciding something not only requires movement but also demands courage to act. Why is it sometimes so hard to act? Why do we often feel frozen in place, unable to take a step forward? I believe it is partly because actions often have permanent results. We might even choose to see those results in our minds as consequences. It is during these moments of indecision when we realize that action needs to occur, that discussion through prayer begins to move from, *"Lord, help me know what to do,"* to *"Lord, help me do what I know I am supposed to do!"*

I guess this is how I felt when I decided to move to Texas. Flying to Fort Worth for an interview in March of 2006 had solidified my decision. But now I had another big decision to make. During my trip to Cambodia, I had met a handsome young man who had captivated my affection and I was afraid had stolen my heart. What was I to do about this new friendship that had been kindled? It was proving to develop into something much more.

When Keith originally invited me on the MANNA trip to Cambodia, he had mentioned that his younger brother would also be joining us on the trip. I knew Keith had two younger brothers, but to be honest, I wasn't sure which brother was which! In my mind, because Keith's younger brothers had both been freshmen during my senior year of high school, they were *much* younger than me and were perhaps still in their late teens or early twenties. (Clearly, I had not done the math right because, even though I had now been divorced for over a year, I was now twenty-five years old!) I didn't think much of what Keith said about his younger brother joining the trip until I saw him.

As I recall, it was like love at first sight, sort of like the movies. I remember seeing Kyle and thinking, *That cannot possibly be Keith's younger brother!* He was twenty-four, not the eighteen-year-old version I had visualized. As Kyle recalls it, I was walking down the rounded staircase at the Phnom Penh Hotel when he saw me and told his friend *"She's mine!"* We spent most of the week in the same group, visiting the various MANNA projects together and playing with the children.

As I watched him interact with the kids at the nutrition centers, I began to see his heart for the needy and downtrodden. I saw selflessness portrayed as he handed out meals to hungry families. He displayed not simply curiosity or even sincere interest but true compassion. I watched while he sat on a bamboo floor and listened to a little boy tell us how he had lost his leg walking through the land mines of the Killing Fields. He kept the picture the little boy drew him, carefully placing it in his journal like a delicate piece of treasure. He still has that picture in his journal to this day. I noticed the shine in his eyes walking through the dust and garbage at the dump as we witnessed the children gathering bits of trash, hoping to salvage whatever they could to sell for a few *riel*. This wasn't simply a vacation for him. Serving these children had impacted his heart, just as it had mine, but in a way that affected his whole demeanor.

I was also thrilled with his apparent love for adventure. It seemed surreal as we rode elephants under a canopy of trees with monkeys jumping from limb to limb on our way to the temple ruins of Angkor Wat. The sun, brimming with the hope of a new day, was just beginning to rise over the tree line, and I felt like I was in a movie. The rest of our team, tired from the long trip, walked through the ruins and then went back to their hotel rooms to rest, but Kyle and I, along with Keith and a few other missionary kids who were part of the team, explored every trail and tunnel we could find. We also managed to find an alligator farm.

Kyle had us all in fits of laughter as he imitated Steve Irwin, the Crocodile Hunter, "*Crikey! Right, so now*

I'm gonna sneak up behind this crocodile." Not wanting to be outdone, my adventurous and competitive nature kicked in. When he sat on the alligator, I bravely followed suit, barely allowing my weight to rest on its rigid back. I wasn't sure I trusted the trainer to keep the alligator from turning around and snapping my legs off. I certainly didn't trust the snake handler when he put the humungous boa around my shoulders. I managed to control my terror long enough for a picture and then grabbed the snake to try and throw it off me.

I happened to turn twenty-six toward the end of our trip to Cambodia. I sat next to Kyle on the airplane ride back to Phnom Penh, after visiting Angkor Wat in Siem Reap. Conversation was easy, and I felt a wave of joy flood over me. We talked about all sorts of topics. What I hadn't realized was that Kyle had arranged for the MANNA team to sing happy birthday to me on the plane ride back. He began, and soon the entire plane erupted into a lively version of "Happy Birthday to You." I was embarrassed to be put on the spot but deeply touched that he had arranged something so bold. When we arrived back in Phnom Penh, a birthday cake was waiting for me at the hotel. I was overwhelmed by this thoughtful gesture and that he had gone to so much effort to make the day special for me. My twenty-sixth birthday was truly one of the most memorable and special birthdays I can remember.

To my dismay, however, I had discovered during our conversations that Kyle lived and worked in the Philippines. Acknowledging to myself that a relationship could never work between us, I knew that when it was time to say goodbye at the end of the ten days, I would probably never see him again. By the end of the trip, however, Kyle had asked for both my email address and my phone number. *What could it hurt?* I thought. He was probably only being polite and would never contact me. I was wrong.

A few weeks after I had returned to Canada, my cell phone rang while I was at work. The caller ID showed a long number that I did not recognize. To my surprise (and absolute delight), I heard a familiar voice on the other line. This began what turned into daily phone calls and emails. Our conversations seemed to pick up right where we had left off in Cambodia. Kyle's thoughtfulness continued to surprise me. One day, I arrived home from work to find a box of beautiful flowers on my doorstep. I had never received flowers in the mail before, and I was overwhelmed, once again, by his genuine care and thoughtfulness.

Who was this man? He knew I was divorced; in fact, he even knew my ex-husband from high school. And yet, he continued to pursue me with gentleness, thoughtfulness, and kindness. He also had an incredible wit. He was quick with his words, beyond funny, but at the same time, nothing about him was superficial. His directness and honesty in our conversations were a breath of fresh air after living in a world where truth was kept at bay. His attention to detail and his love for nature also interested me.

I was surprised that he not only had a dog but also kept plants in his apartment in the Philippines. I'm not exactly sure why that was a surprise, but to me, it reiterated the fact that he cared about, and for, delicate things, living things. Kyle was a mystery and yet an open book. This irony captivated me.

And so, there were two decisions that I carefully and prayerfully made: my move to Texas to begin work for MANNA Worldwide and the decision to carry on a long-distance relationship with a man I had not only just recently met but who also happened to live in not only a different time zone but also on a different continent! Would these worlds ever come together? Even though I wasn't sure if my decision to join MANNA would ever coincide with my decision to have a long-distance relationship with Kyle, I knew it was time to act and begin the process of leaving Canada.

I had very few belongings, so I knew that they wouldn't be hard to move. I stored my college textbooks, papers, and childhood memorabilia in my parents' shed and then sold what little furniture I had: a wooden futon that I used as my bed, a small table and two chairs, and a dresser. My piano was the most difficult item I had to part with, not only because I had just paid it off and it was completely mine but also because, for me, it had symbolized a new start. Aside from my car, this was the only major purchase I had made on my own since my divorce. I had also spent hundreds of hours teaching and practicing this instrument. I recognize that a piano is an inanimate piece of furniture, an item that can be replaced, and while the lady who bought it seemed like she would play it often and take good care of it, I still felt like a piece of me was rolling out the door with the piano. The remainder of my belongings were packed into several boxes and duffel bags. What I couldn't fit into my two-door Honda Civic was put on a truck bound for Texas.

Somehow, I managed to pack my little Civic full and save enough space for me and my loyal friends, Corrie and Natasha, to squeeze in. Together, Corrie and I meticulously planned our route. Back in the "olden times" (my children like to give this special title to any time period before their birth), before smartphones and GPS, we used *Yahoo!* to plot our journey and then printed out each page of directions to make sure we arrived on time to check in to the Motel 6 we had reserved.

Good old Rand McNally[106] was also never far from reach so that whoever was navigating would have easy access to all the maps for every state we drove through. We knew it would be a long drive to Fort Worth, about five thousand kilometers, and all three of us would need to take turns driving. So in the weeks before we left, I taught Natasha how to drive a 5-speed.

Natasha is an amazing, gracious, and kind woman, with a wit sharper than a knife. But put her in a stick shift in the middle of traffic and day four of our road trip became a day I will never forget! Corrie and I woke up to shouts for help from Natasha. She had stalled in the middle of rush hour traffic on an overpass somewhere in downtown Albuquerque. I'm sure the other cars on the freeway were wondering what was happening as we managed to complete a Chinese fire drill dance around the car. With everyone switching spots, we were all back in the car and ready to roll before the car in front of us even moved! (I'm not quite sure why all of us were required to change spots, but somehow, during the panic, we all seemed to shuffle around, and I ended up back in the driver's seat.) After that, Natasha said she would only drive on the rural roads in Idaho!

I have so many great memories from that five-day road trip. Jamming to the great classics of U2 and Coldplay, we cruised through more than seven states. We had deep and meaningful conversations, cracked hilarious jokes, and laughed until our bellies hurt. True friend-

---
[106] Rand McNally Road Atlas.

ship is about sacrifice, and I believe Corrie and Natasha both sacrificed much on that trip, sleep being one of those things!

The night we camped on the ridge of the Grand Canyon was by far the most memorable. Cold and uncomfortable, we huddled together in our tent, eating a bag of nacho chips for dinner, mesmerized by the beauty of God's creation. Witnessing both the sunset and the sunrise over the south rim of the Grand Canyon was truly a spectacular sight that I'm sure none of us will ever forget.

In 2004, Brian Doerksen wrote a powerful song that conveys the awe and wonder I felt. *"How can I say there is no God, when all around creation calls?"*[107] The expanse of the Grand Canyon revealed to me both God's startling creativity and immense power. If He could create such an awe-inspiring landscape, how much more could He create in the way of a new home for me in Texas?

> Lord, our Lord, how majestic is your name in all the earth! You have set your glory in the heavens. When I consider your heavens, the work of your fingers, the moon and the stars, which you have set in place, what is man that you are mindful of him, the son of man that you care for him?[108]

And so, I began to notice little blessings along the way, glimpses of God's goodness and reminders of His

---

[107] Brian Doerksen, "Creation Calls," Track #10 on *Today*, Hosanna! Music, 2004, compact disc.
[108] Psalm 8:1, 3–4 (NIV).

promised faithfulness. God had already answered so many of my prayers regarding the details in preparing for my move. When I look back on all the practical things that needed to happen, I realize that the Lord looked after me and prepared the way for me.

As a dual citizen, I was able to simply drive my car across the border without having to pay any taxes on it. Although hard to part with, the Lord arranged a buyer for my piano, the sale of which provided me with the funds I needed for the move. Dear friends supported my decision to move and encouraged me to dream big. Corrie, Natasha, and I arrived safely in Fort Worth without getting lost or having any mishaps: no flat tires, no mechanical issues with my car, no accidents or even close calls, and no speeding tickets!

My church, too, had sent me on my way with their blessings and prayers. After giving a presentation about my trip to Cambodia and my decision to join MANNA Worldwide, there were even a few members who graciously and sacrificially committed to supporting me financially. Although my job description at MANNA Worldwide had not yet been specifically defined, these loving individuals had willingly offered to support my new role, whatever it would be. I was deeply honored and humbled.

My decision to join MANNA Worldwide seemed as big as the decision my parents had made to join Wycliffe Bible Translators so many years ago. I imagine they had felt the same thrill mixed with trepidation that I felt. True, I was moving to a new country where my future was a little unsure (and certainly the culture in Texas was different from anywhere else I had ever lived), but they had literally moved across the world to not only a new country but also to a new continent!

Smartphones were not readily accessible until about 2008, but I at least had a cell phone (remember the Motorola Razr flip phone?). My parents, on the other hand, relied on a single-sideband radio to send messages to their coworkers, and letters home were sent by boat (airmail letters cost more). Unlike my parents, I had full use of the Internet, air-conditioning in my apartment, and access to a washing machine and dryer. They washed their clothes in a freshwater spring and dried them on a clothesline. I suppose our adventures did have a few things in common though. We both drove small, gray cars with a stick shift and windows that you had to manually roll up!

All jokes aside, the point I am making is that it doesn't really matter where God calls you or how far away God calls you. What matters is that you are obedient by taking one step at a time in the direction in which you hear His voice calling. He might even be calling you to have a cup of coffee with a neighbor across the street, and that might feel like the scariest thing you have been asked to do in a long time! Sometimes what He asks you to do may seem easy, and other times, it may take what might seem like all your time, all your resources, and all your energy. For my parents, they even gave up their youth so that the Ibatan people from Babuyan Island would have the very words of God in their own language.

I believe there are times when the Lord provides several choices, all of which can sometimes be the right choice. He gives us the freedom to evaluate which one would be best for our lives, but more importantly, He gives us the opportunity to seek Him for the best decision. We can certainly make decisions on our own, but if we choose to pray and ask for wisdom, direction, guidance, and discernment, how much more confident will we be in our decision? We can struggle through the decision-making process on our own, but if we know that we are not alone and that we have help, that is comforting! And then there are also times when there is only one clear decision to be made. Do we have the courage to take one step of faith at a time, asking for the Lord's wisdom for each step we take?

At the time that the decision of joining MANNA was presented to me, I had just been accepted into the MA TESOL program at Trinity Western University. I believe that had I stayed in Canada to complete my graduate studies, that would have been an excellent decision. However, I would have missed out on so much more had I not chosen to move to Texas. I chose to follow what I felt deep in my spirit that God was calling me to do. A risk, a leap of faith, a challenge? Call it what you would like to, but after the discussion process with my friends, family, and spiritual mentors and spending much time in prayer, I have had no regrets about the decision I made to withdraw from graduate school and make the move the Texas.

We can have the best ideas for how we see our future unfolding, but when God presents a new option, we need to be willing to listen, pray for discernment, and then boldly step into action. As Joshua was preparing to cross into the promised land and take possession of it, Moses reminded him that *"the Lord himself goes before you and will be with you; he will never leave you nor forsake you. Do not be afraid; do not be discouraged."*[109]

However, I must admit that I did sort of feel like the J. R. R. Tolkien character Bilbo Baggins from *The Hobbit* at times. How on earth had I managed to leave a perfectly good job (three jobs, in fact), sell my means of livelihood (my piano), and drive thousands of kilometers to another country? I wasn't sure where I was going to live, how much money I would be earning, or even what my job title was. While I knew I had made the right decision, I felt unprepared, ill-equipped, and yet wildly excited for what lay ahead. Perhaps this is why my dad gave me the nickname the Great Belladonna Took, or Tookie for short. The fictitious character created by J. R. R. Tolkien, the Belladonna Took was the mother of Bilbo Baggins. She had a great adventurous spirit, unlike the standard personalities displayed by the other Hobbits, which led her to remarkable exploits. When Bilbo's "Tookish" side took over, he found himself on the adventure of a lifetime.

> To the end of his days Bilbo could never remember how he found himself outside, without a hat, a walking-stick or any money, or anything that he usually took when he went out; leaving his second breakfast half-finished and quite unwashed-up, pushing his keys into Gandalf's hands, and running as fast as his furry feet could carry him down the lane, past the great Mill,

---
[109] Deuteronomy 31:8 (NIV).

across The Water, and then on for a mile or more.[110]

In those moments when fear and excitement mingle, adventure awaits. There was a stirring within me, a restlessness to follow the path of adventure to Fort Worth. Perhaps, like Bilbo, the Tookish side of me took over. What I actually believe to be true is that the Holy Spirit, living in me, breathed life, hope, and a sense of adventure into my soul. While not every person might have agreed with my decision to join MANNA Worldwide and move to Texas, I knew in my heart that I had to at least start the adventure. I knew I could always come back home, but what I was excited to find out was if I would be able to create a new home, one in which I felt I was serving, helping, and spreading the Gospel to marginalized children and their families around the world. If I could somehow be a small part of this endeavor, then I knew I could be at home wherever that adventure took me.

At the end of his epic journey to reclaim the kingdom of Erebor from Smaug, the terrifying dragon, Bilbo, realized that *"he was in fact held by all the hobbits of the neighbourhood to be 'queer'—except by his nephews and nieces on the Took side."*[111] I, too, might be held by many to be odd, impulsive, or even unwise. And yet, for those who have let their Tookish side take over, who have heard the Holy Spirit whisper into their hearts, it is a call to embark on an epic journey of trust in the faithfulness of God. It is about stepping out in faith and obedience to follow where the Lord is leading.

---

[110] J. R. R. Tolkien, *The Hobbit* (Hammersmith: HarperCollins Publishers, 1999), 29.
[111] J.R.R. Tolkien, *The Hobbit*, 278.

Perhaps we can learn to be content in this obedience, and like Bilbo, we won't mind what others say because we will be at peace knowing we followed the Spirit's call.

> He was quite content; and the sound of the kettle on the hearth was ever after more musical than it had been even in the quiet days before the Unexpected Party...and though few believed any of his tales, he remained very happy to the end of his days, and those were extraordinarily long.[112]

---

[112] J.R.R. Tolkien, *The Hobbit*, 278.

Eleven

Texas Heat

Trust in the Lord with all your heart and lean not on your own understanding; in all your ways acknowledge him and he will make your paths straight.

Proverbs 3:5–6

There comes a time when you must look back at the decisions you made and remember why you made them in the first place. The third *D* from "Dad's three *D*s" is the word *determine*. We have all heard the old American English witticism that says, *"When the going gets tough, the tough get going."* I suppose this is true for the determination part of the three *D*s. When the excitement of the decision-making process has worn off, what is now required is the determination to see the decision through.

Webster defines *determination* as "the act of deciding definitely and firmly" as well as a "firm or fixed intention to achieve a desired end."[113] What stands out to me in these definitions is the word *firm*, which conjures up for

---

[113] https://www.merriam-webster.com/dictionary/determination.

me images of steadfastness, a definitive resoluteness, and an unwavering stance. I will be the first to admit that I have absolutely wavered in many of my decisions after they were made, that I have second-guessed my decisions (multiple times), and that I doubted if I had the resolve to carry through with the decisions I had previously made. I am pretty sure, however, that I am not the only one who has ever had these uncertainties arise and that I am also not the only one who has ever cried out to the Lord for the determination to follow through on a decision I have made.

Numerous verses in the Bible speak not only of the Lord's graciousness to give courage and strength to those who need it but also of the promise to never abandon the one seeking help. *"Be strong and courageous. Do not be afraid or terrified of them, for the Lord your God goes with you; he will never leave you nor forsake you."*[114] While this verse is in reference to Joshua's imminent battle to conquer the promised land, this verse is true for us today.

The Lord grants us strength and courage when we seek His face so that we do not have to live in the "spirit of fear." Instead, we can boldly move forward, knowing that we are not alone in the battle and that we have been given the resources we need to overcome our fear: the spirit of "power and of love and of a sound mind."[115] How encouraging to know that we are not only equipped but also are not alone! It's one thing for a friend to give you the tools you need to complete a daunting task, but it's a completely different story for that friend to also lend a hand.

---

[114] Deuteronomy 31:6 (NIV).
[115] 2 Timothy 1:7 (NIV).

When circumstances get tough, when the heat is on, it's easy to complain and blame others, ourselves, and even God for our present conditions. Often, the difficult circumstances we find ourselves in are because of our own poor decisions. There are times, however, when we have encountered opposition and difficulty even when we have made a good decision through much deliberation and prayer. We feel alone and vulnerable even when we believe we stepped out in faith and obedience to do what the Lord asked us to do.

My dear dad has reminded me through the years that even during these trying times, we have much hope to cling to. "Don't doubt in the dark what God has already shown you in the light," he would tell me, quoting V. R. Edman. The Lord's promises are just as true in the tough times as they are in the good times. His goodness and faithfulness are not determined by our circumstances. That would diminish His sovereignty. God is God, and His promises remain.

Numbers 23:19 says of the Lord, "*God is not a man, so he does not lie. He is not human, so he does not change his mind. Has he ever spoke and failed to act? Has he ever promised and not carried it through?*" When we claim God's promises, we can rest knowing with full assurance that He will fulfill them.

Hebrews 6:18 says, "*So God has given both his promise and his oath. These two things are unchangeable because it is impossible for God to lie. Therefore, we who have fled to him for refuge can have great confidence as we hold to the hope that lies before us.*" I love the way the New Living Translation phrases this verse. It describes the Lord as a refuge, a sanctuary that we can run to once we have escaped the spirit of fear that Timothy condemns. The

Lord is a shelter and a place of safety that provides restorative healing, assurance, and hope for the future.

Being a recipient of what this haven offers, however, requires action: "*We who have fled to him for refuge.*" We must run away from the fear that threatens to drown us and boldly cling to the "*hope that lies before us,*" Who, indeed, is Christ the Lord. It requires a decision to turn from the anxiety, sorrow, and loneliness that hold us captive and embrace the promise of hope that is our certain future.

Moving to Texas left me feeling both exhilarated and apprehensive. Once I arrived in Fort Worth, I wondered if I would be able to settle into life in Texas as easily as I had imagined in my head. I clung to the Lord for refuge as I began to navigate my new life in a new country, but it was not easy. I arrived in Fort Worth at the end of July, right in the middle of summer, and began work at the MANNA office in August. (If you have ever spent a summer in Texas, you will know what I mean when I say, "the middle of summer." With temperatures soaring well over one hundred degrees Fahrenheit, it was hot!)

Within a few months, I was preparing for my first international trip to the countries of Kenya and Tanzania. Bruce and Pam O'Neal were leading this trip, taking a church group from Wisconsin to visit MANNA's projects in Mombasa, and I was happy to be taking my first trip as a staff member with them. Although I would not be traveling to Zimbabwe or South Africa, the countries where many of my father's relatives still lived, I was thrilled to be able to visit the continent that my dad had spent the formative years of his life calling home.

When we arrived at Bomani, the first center we visited, I was overwhelmed to the point of tears as we drove through the gate, leaving dozens of children outside clambering for our attention. These were the children who either did not qualify for our feeding and education program or were on the waiting list. We simply did not have enough staff, space, or resources to feed the growing number of children left outside the walled-in facility. I was heartbroken. Seeing my tears and moved to compassion, Bruce helped me climb on top of the cement wall. Together, we threw out handfuls of candy to the cheering children down below. Later, Bruce explained to me that the plan was always to help more children. Even if the children were not able to attend our school, the missionaries still had a strong presence in the community surrounding our facility. I was momentarily reassured, but I still felt as though I had simply put a small Band-Aid on an oversized, festering wound.

Spending time at our centers in Africa gave me a better insight into the work that MANNA did overseas. Feeding children is essential. Have you ever fasted? Try fasting for even just one day, depriving your body of the nutrients it needs to feel healthy and function well. Anyone who has fasted for any length of time will tell you that the hunger one experiences becomes all-consuming. Imagine if you were hungry, but instead of denying yourself food for whatever the reason might be (diet for weight loss, spiritual fasting, and the like), you simply had no food to eat.

While this is not a new concept, MANNA found that combining nutrition with education not only helped gain the trust of the children's parents but also provided inroads into the community for a more long-lasting, sustainable presence. If the children were no longer hungry and were given the opportunity for an education, the parents were much more willing to investigate what the church had to say about the Bible, and there was always an open invitation for parents to attend the local church. MANNA was, in essence, modeling what the church was preaching.

While I was ecstatic about my recent trip to Africa and about my upcoming trip to Romania and Hungary, I was still finding the move to Texas difficult. I had left my friends, my family, my church, job security, and grad school, and to top it all off, I was alone. I was struggling to meet people my age and to make friends, and that left me desperately lonely. I had prayerfully considered my move and felt confident that the Lord had led me to work for MANNA Worldwide, but the transition was not easy. I was also struggling financially.

Although I had spent my first few months bouncing back and forth between living in the Hallmark Baptist Church (now known as Hallmark Church) missionary apartment housing and the upstairs suite at Bruce and Pam's house (for which I am extremely grateful), I was now settled in a small, one-bedroom, five-hundred-square-foot apartment. This, of course, required rent to be paid on time each month. I had sold my piano and anything else of monetary value before I had left Canada, including my engagement ring, wedding band, and wedding dress, but I was still reeling from the aftereffects of paying for a divorce. The separation itself had left me with some debt that I was doing my utmost to pay off. The end was in sight, and by my calculations, with my current meager employment, I only had about four or five years to go until I was debt-free.

I realized, however, that I would need additional income to not only make ends meet but also to pay off my debt sooner. To make that happen, I would need to find another job. In the end, I ended up with three additional jobs! In this way, the Lord continued to faithfully provide for me.

I am grateful to Hallmark Baptist Church for offering me a position as their church pianist. This entailed accompanying the congregation during worship for two services on Sunday mornings, most Sunday evening services, and an occasional choir rehearsal on Wednesday nights. I had been quite involved at my church in Canada, playing on a worship team, and I welcomed the chance to once again play in a worship band. I even had the opportunity to play for a few funerals, as I had done in Canada. This all made me feel more at home, and I was happy to have the chance to play the piano even though I no longer owned one.

Soon, church members began asking if I taught piano lessons. I knew that this was not my focus, but I said I could teach a few students. So after I finished work at the MANNA office in the late afternoons, I began to teach a few students at the church. This eventually turned into several full afternoons of teaching, including a part-time job teaching at a local music school. It was at this school that I met a sweet lady by the name of Jennifer, who became one of my dear friends. She was also a music teacher, and we bonded instantly.

I am so thankful to the Lord for providing such a sweet friend who not only shared my love for music but also my desire to grow deeper in my relationship with Jesus. Her friendship encouraged me during this difficult season of my life and has continued to spur me on to pursue Christ in my everyday life to this day.

My next job was being a ticket sales agent at the Modern Art Museum of Fort Worth. How I got this job was a miracle. In the Lord's deep love for me, He provided another true friend who happened to work there: Tiffany. We were both grappling with difficult circumstances, but somehow, we found a way to encourage each other through the bleakness of the season we were going through.

Tiffany had just started grad school and was struggling to make ends meet as I was, but she had a drive and determination that reminded me so much of Marlaena, my dear friend from Canada. To top it all off, she was a fellow MK (missionary kid) from the Philippines who, like me, had also attended Faith Academy as a dorm student. We were instant friends. Was it a coincidence? Maybe, but I choose to believe it was God's kindness and provision for me that He gave me the gift of meeting Tiffany.

I can remember long, drawn-out days selling tickets to museum-goers over the weekend and countless late nights sitting in coat check with Tiffany. We lamented over the trials we were facing but at the same time laughed together over the ridiculousness of where we were. We would dream big, hoping to leave in the wee hours of the morning with our tip jar overflowing with loose change and perhaps a few bills from the overintoxicated wedding guests. Knowing that I had to play the piano for the early service in just a few hours, I would pray that the guests would leave so I could go home to bed.

As if working weekends at the museum wasn't enough, I had also begun working for a local company that conducted estate sales in the area. Having to stand for hours and walk around a house packed with items for sale to make sure nothing went missing was exhausting. What made it worthwhile was the group of people I got to work with. At the end of the day, we would wearily sink into whatever seats had not yet been sold and chuckle over the grumpy salegoers. We would swap stories about those who impatiently pushed past other shoppers, determined to be first in line to claim the merchandise it seemed they couldn't live without.

I have pleasant memories of this great bunch of individuals, who, in a way, gave me a sense of belonging in Fort Worth. I grew to know the area better as I drove around the city to work at these various estate sales. I learned the history of who had lived in the homes we worked in and discovered that, in many ways, Fort Worth was a close-knit community. While I continued to battle the restlessness of living between worlds and cultures, I slowly began to feel more settled in Fort Worth.

If you were counting the hours of the day, you might have begun to run out of time with all the jobs I had acquired. It certainly seemed like that at times. I felt exhausted and spread thin, running on very few hours of sleep at night and spending my days going from one job to the next. Even the weekends provided no reprieve, as they were often busier than the weekdays. To top it all off, even though Kyle had moved from the Philippines back to Fort Worth just a few months before I had arrived in Texas, he had once again taken a job back in the Philippines and planned to live there for several months.

Once more, we were subjected to a long-distance relationship, a relationship that I was beginning to become anxious about. How long would Kyle work overseas? Was there a future for us? Since Kyle was the son of Bruce and Pam, I knew that if our relationship ended, it would make it very difficult for me to continue working for MANNA. Perhaps it would be better to return to Canada, to my old job, to my friends and family. MANNA surely didn't need me. In the short time I had been with MANNA, they had grown and had hired more staff members and directors. It had been nearly three years since I had moved to Texas, and there would be no shame now in going home. As much as I had begun to feel at home in Fort Worth, I began to wonder if perhaps it was time for me to return to Canada.

I kept going back to the decision I had made in March of 2006. I rehearsed in my mind the many ways in which the Lord had guided me, the confirmations He had given me, and His continued reassurance that He was with me. If I truly believed that the Lord was with me and that He had guided my decision to move to Texas, then no matter how difficult circumstances got, I knew I could rely on His faithfulness and trust that He would never leave me.

Philippians 4:6 says, *"Do not be anxious about anything, but in every situation, by prayer and petition, with thanksgiving, present your requests to God."* How freeing to know that there was nothing that I should let overwhelm me. God's promise was that, in "every situation," I could call on him. The beautiful part about this verse is that when my requests were presented to the Lord with a pure heart, a thankful heart, I was promised *"the peace of God, which transcends all understanding."*[116]

I'm sure you will agree with me that the "presenting the requests" part of this verse is easy to do. It's the "with thanksgiving" part that is much more difficult! Could I

---

[116] Philippians 4:7 (NIV).

be truly thankful for the jobs the Lord had provided for me, despite how exhausted I felt trying to successfully work all of them? Could I give God the glory for providing deep, lasting friendships? Could I praise God for the opportunity I had to meet Kyle, along with his generous and kind family, even if the future of our relationship was undecided? Could I give God the glory for the way He had led me to Texas, allowing me to visit multiple countries and serve the children of his kingdom?

If so, what then was the purpose of allowing myself to succumb to the fear of the unknown or to the anxiety of my overwhelming schedule? If Kyle and I were not meant to move forward with our relationship, then I would have to trust the Lord that His timing would be perfect and that He would take care of me regardless of whether or not Kyle and I had a future together.

I had to trust that working three or four jobs would not always be the story of my life. One day, if I was diligent and responsible with what the Lord had given me, then I would be free from debt, free from the constraints of working so many hours, and free to financially bless others, which I was unable to do at the present time.

Reading through the Psalms one day, I discovered a verse in Psalm 31 that sank into the deepest recesses of my heart. *"You have not handed me over to the enemy but have set my feet in a spacious place."* Underlining it, I wrote in the margins, "*1/2/08 Texas.*" Little did I know how spacious Texas really was! (Everything really is bigger in Texas!)

My mother's favorite song is "Great Is Thy Faithfulness," which has become a theme song in my life as well. During difficult times in my life where I have begun to turn inward, taking an introspective look at the world (i.e., more of a self-centered, "poor me" type of approach), I would recall the words to this profound hymn. "*Great is thy faithfulness, O God my Father. There is no shadow of turning with Thee. Thou changest not, thy compassions, they fail not. Great is thy faithfulness, Lord unto me.*"[117] The hymn continues through several verses, a personal declaration of God's goodness in comparison to our inadequacy, our frailty, our sin. The chorus, woven in between the verses, reveals the steadfastness of the Lord in a final restatement of His mighty faithfulness. "*All I have needed Thy hand hath provided. Great is Thy faithfulness, Lord unto me.*"

I was not naive enough to think that moving to Texas to join MANNA Worldwide would be completely smooth sailing. I knew what it would entail. I had calculated the cost and taken the leap, but there were still challenges that I was learning to overcome. In her book *Becoming a Woman of Influence*, Carol Kent asks a profound question: "*What happens when you catch a vision of what God might be doing in your life and then you act on that dream?*" She responds by saying that you not only experience risk, fear, and total dependence on God, but on the flip side, you also experience joy. Kent goes on to say that the Christian life is "*never static.*" Choices will continually need to be brought before the Father, and His wisdom will always need to be sought after. This thought was refreshing to me. I had not yet arrived. I had much to learn, and I was only at the beginning of this incredible journey. Kent's honest reflection resonated well with me.

---

[117] Thomas Obadiah Chisholm.

> I know my life is a journey, and at times I think I've arrived at the place of influence God wants me to be in for the rest of my life. Then I look at the landscape and see the faces of people I've met along the way—people who need compassion, unconditional love…and I realize…the more I look at the example of Christ, the more I get a vision of the new challenges He has for me.[118]

How could I daily pursue the vision that He had called me to? Even if I wasn't daily feeding impoverished children on the mission field in a foreign country, I could still live in the joy of knowing that I was doing what the Lord had called me to do. If He was faithful to provide, to sustain, and to uphold me, could I not be faithful in the daily tasks that He had asked me to do? Even when I knew that God's faithfulness would follow me no matter where I went, I still sometimes had doubts that I was in the place that God had called me to. In fact, even today, in my frailty and sin, when I am downcast and alone, I can begin to doubt that God will fulfill His promises to me. It is a journey that I am still on today, a journey of learning to let go of my fear and trusting in God's character. And yet each time I begin to doubt His faithfulness, I am reminded of what it says in Lamentations: "Because of the Lord's great love we are not consumed, for his compassions never fail. They are new every morning; great is your faithfulness."[119]

---

[118] Carol Kent, Becoming a Woman of Influence: Making a Lasting Impact on Others (Colorado Springs: NavPress, 1999), 174, 177.
[119] Lamentations 3:22–23 (NIV)

Twelve

Adventure Is Out There![120]

You make known to me the path of life; you will fill me with joy in your presence, with eternal pleasures at your right hand.

Psalm 16:11

I have always had an affinity for adventure. Call it what you will—exploration, investigation, curiosity, *tookishness*, or just daring to seek something new, this is what makes life exciting! I suppose this began at an early age since my parents involved us in all their adventures in the Philippines. I don't think they ever intended any of their escapades to be thrill seeking, but they were certainly adventurous.

Living on Babuyan, a volcanic, tropical island, there were endless opportunities for adventure. The joke my parents always told was that we had running water in our house, you just had to run and get it. True story. When my sister and I were old enough (around seven or eight

---

[120] *UP.* Directed by Pete Docter and Bob Peterson, Walt Disney Pictures, 2009.

years old), we were tasked with the responsibility of taking the dirty laundry and dishes to the *oksong* (freshwater spring). We were never to go down to the *oksong* empty-handed, so when we didn't have laundry or dishes to wash, we each took containers (empty, two-gallon plastic cooking oil containers that we had saved and cleaned) to fill up with drinking water.

The Ibatan are very particular about their water. The freshwater spring is nearly ice-cold, bubbling straight out of a rock. It is pure, clear, delicious, and absolutely as refreshing (if not more) than any three-dollar bottle of spring water you can purchase at the store. I remember there being an unwritten rule regarding the use of the water at the *oksong* that all the Ibatan were familiar with, a type of hierarchy to water usage. The water at the source was sectioned off for drinking water. Only containers to be filled for drinking water were allowed here. Farther down, dishes were washed and rinsed, and where the spring opens up into a large, hand-dug pool was where clothes were washed and people were allowed to bathe. Outside this sectioned-off area was a watering hole for the animals.

The *oksong* was a lovely place to be, especially in the heat of the summer. It was only about a five- to ten-minute walk from our house down a jungle path to get there, but by the time you reached home again, you were covered once more in a blanket of sweat, and your feet were filthy, coated with the black, powdery volcanic soil. And so, my father's idea for a water distribution system was brilliant. He had an elaborate plan to build a potable water system so that more people on the island had access to water. The trouble was that he needed to investigate whether or not it would be possible to pipe the water through mountains of rock, a jungle, and then down the side of a volcano to the people at sea level. And so, each summer, when my sister and I came home from boarding school, my parents planned some type of family hiking trip to help my dad map out the land for his water distribution system.

On these trips, my dad would research sources of water and the possibilities of how to pipe water from the freshwater springs that bubbled out of the lava rock at the top of the mountain to sea level. At the time, there were some families, even though they used their carabaos (water buffalos) to carry their drinking water, who would walk long distances to get to the water spring. My dad succeeded, by the way, and today many, many people on the island have much closer access to running water than they had in previous years before.

During these exploration hikes, we found ourselves climbing two different active volcanos. We always had a group of Ibatan friends with us. Most were simply curious about the volcanos, as they had never been to the top of these volcanos themselves. But I'm sure others were even more curious about why we would willingly spend our free time hiking. They did this every day, hiking through the jungle to get water, to work in the fields, or to visit the neighbors. Why on earth would you want to do this for fun in your spare time?

The first volcano that we climbed together as a family was *Chinteb a Wasay* (*Chinteb* for short), or quite literally, "The Cut of an Ax." This is because the crater at the top of the three-thousand-five-hundred-foot volcano was shaped as if an ax had taken away a huge portion of it. I was about fourteen years old at the time of this family expedition. My sister and I had just completed our first year of boarding school, and we were spending our summer break on Babuyan. After many hours of walking (in flip-flops) to the base of the volcano, we began our ascent through the thick jungle. We were always on the lookout for *marem*, the deadly, poisonous green vipers that are almost undetectable in their natural habitat. I had heard stories and had even seen evidence of those who had been bitten by a *marem*, and it was not something I wanted to add to my list of personal experiences. Needless to say, we spent a restless night on the slope of *Gerger* (another smaller volcano at the base of *Chinteb*).

Early the next morning and after a hurried breakfast, we reached the summit of *Chinteb*. We were exhausted. Trying to make our way around the edge of the massive crater seemed nearly impossible because of the long elephant grass. At times, the narrow edge of the crater we were walking along was not much wider than our feet, and we were forced to walk (very carefully, I might add) single file. We eventually realized this was far too dangerous and that there wasn't enough time to go around the crater before dark. So we thought of an alternative route that involved descending into the crater itself. Most of us in the group were for this; however, no one had ever been inside the crater, and we had no idea if there were any smaller craters located beneath the dense vegetation that might pose a threat to us.

After much discussion, the consensus was to continue walking precariously and quite slowly around the edge of the outer crater. However, while the decision was being made, some of the group (including myself) had already started descending the slope into the crater. I accidentally fell and slid several feet down the slope of the crater while trying to follow those ahead of me. It was too difficult for me to climb back to the top, so the rest of the crew decided to abandon the original plan of walking around the rim of the crater and continued the downward climb, following us to the center of the crater. We all prayed the ground would be solid as we trekked through what seemed like the center of the earth.

As we began walking, I realized I was having difficulty seeing, and my vision was blurry, especially on one side. As it turns out, I had somehow lost a contact during my fall. For the remaining time that it took us to walk through the crater, then back to our camp, and finally home again, I wore one contact. By the time we reached home, I had a headache, but the adventure had been worth it! The view from the top of the volcano was breathtaking. You could see the jungle cascading all the way down the side of the mountain, right to the choppy waves in the ocean below. I marveled at God's creation, knowing that only a God with artistry and imagination could create a world so majestic.

The following year, in 1995, my parents organized another family hiking expedition. This time, we planned to climb the volcano on the far western side of Babuyan Island. This volcano was called *Pokis* because of its cinder cone top. In the trade language of Ilocano, *pokis* means *haircut*. I suppose the name fits because hardly any vegetation grew on this volcano. Unlike *Chinteb a Wasay*, which had foliage, this volcano was covered in crumbling lava rock and sand, which were hot to walk on.

Even though we had waited to start our trek up the volcano until 3:00 p.m., when we thought the sun would not be so hot, it felt like we were baking in an oven under the scorching sun. We started from our campsite at sea level and began the arduous walk up the face of the mountain, intending to make it to the top and straight down the other side in one hour, hoping to be back at camp before sunset. We wanted to carry as little as possible in the heat, so we had nothing with us—no water, no food, and no flashlights. (In hindsight, we might have been a little overzealous with our initial plan!)

Since vegetation was scarce, there was little to grab hold of, so it was a struggle to climb up the face of the mountain, especially as loose rocks were continually being dislodged by climbers ahead of us, tumbling down on top of us. Halfway up the climb, my dad, who had recently had back surgery from a very serious accident, and my sister, who was not feeling well, turned back. My mother and I, however, continued with our group of Ibatan friends to face the challenge of climbing up to the summit. We were all thirsty and longed for water. Knowing that the other side of the mountain had more vegetation, we persevered and finally reached the summit by about 6:00 p.m. (So much for going up and down in an hour!)

As night fell and it became dark, we realized that none of us had brought a flashlight! While the stars were brilliant in the night sky, it was quite dark; and as you can imagine, we were a little apprehensive about making it back to our camp without any source of light. Together, we figured out which direction we should be heading to get back to our camp and made a beeline for it. Eventually, we saw a flicker of light in the direction we were heading. The other group with my dad and sister had made it successfully back to our camp but had sent a small search party with a Coleman lantern to look for us when it got dark. When we finally did make it back to camp around 8:30 p.m., it was completely dark, and we were exhausted, ready for a hot dinner and a soft bed. We got a hot dinner, but the soft bed was probably too much to ask for on the side of a mountain.

When we weren't spending the summers climbing volcanos on Babuyan, our family planned other fun outings around the town of Bagabag. My dad had realized that getting around the local area and the nearby town on the main island of Luzon would be much easier and cheaper on a motorcycle. On the weekends, Dad often took us all on the 250-cc Suzuki trail bike riding around the back country roads and rolling hills of the Bagabag valley, or down to a river not too far from our home. When we were still young children, our whole family managed to fit on this one motorcycle: my dad driving, my mom behind him, and my sister and I in front of him. We would pack a picnic lunch and spend the day playing at the river with family friends. I always looked forward to these river trips because, to me, they were like mini vacations.

I was about five years old on the way home one day from such an adventure. According to my dad, the throttle jammed on the motorcycle heading downhill on a curvy road. I recall this narrow path to be gravel, banked on one side with a steep drop-off on the other. To avoid plummeting over the steep cliff (to what my five-year-old mind was sure to be certain death), my dad steered the motorcycle into the side of the embankment, away from the cliff. With his leg holding up the motorcycle, he had just enough time to grab my seven-year-old sister, who was sitting in front of him, and throw her off onto a patch of grass. I was sitting in front of my sister on the gas tank. Before he could get me off, something snapped in his ankle, a possible broken bone. The result was that my face was ground into the side of the mountain as the motorcycle climbed the embankment and fell backward. Fortunately, my dad was able to throw his arm in front of my face to cover my eyes before we contacted the mountain. My dad consequently lost much of the skin on the back of his forearm. My mother, who was sitting behind my dad, injured the back of her leg when she was thrown off the motorcycle. None of us were wearing helmets.

Despite the obvious danger of climbing a volcanic mountain in flip-flops with absolutely no gear or traveling with a family of four on a motorcycle, these adventurous summer activities were a highlight for me. It was a wonderful time for building memories—incidents that my family refers to as *"family bonding."*

I enjoyed not only the physical activity, pushing our bodies to the limits of what was doable in flip-flops and intense tropical heat, but also the thrill of doing something that bordered on danger! As you can imagine, I grew up with a unique picture of what a vacation might look like. Suntanning on a white sand beach was not on the list of vacations we typically took together as a family! (There was an incident at a beach, however, that involved an attempt at sailing, a missing oar, and nearly being lost at sea without any life jackets! Fortunately, my ever-resourceful dad managed to figure out how to get us back to shore without any injuries.)

Every four years, my family left the Philippines for a planned, year-long furlough in North America. We spent most of the year in Canada (either in Calgary, Alberta, or in the Langley, British Columbia, area, which was close to my father's family), but we would often begin our furlough in San Francisco, spending a month or so with my mother's family. My parents would plan our travel to

North America with an intentional stopover (otherwise known as vacation) in some country along the way, like Japan or Singapore.

Breaking up our travel, we would spend a day or two exploring the city, traveling by public transportation, and trying out the local food. As adventurous as we were, none of us ever did develop a taste for durian. If you have ever eaten durian, you will almost certainly remember the experience! Durian is a favorite tropical fruit in South East Asia that is similar in looks to jackfruit. Durian, however, has a more pasty, custardy-type texture on the inside and a distinctly pungent smell. Both the flavor and the smell are hard to ignore and remain evident on a person's breath for a lengthy period! (In some countries, durian is even banned in public spaces because of its overpowering smell!) For some reason, my dad was always sure that he had picked "a bad one," convincing himself that "the next one" would taste better. The verdict is still out on that one!

I will always be grateful to my parents for taking us with them on their explorations, giving us rare and wonderful experiences as well as the opportunity to see the world. Together, we have traveled to over a dozen countries.

For our furlough trip home to Canada in 1986, when I was six years old, Granny and Grandpa Maree, my father's parents, had asked us to join them on a trip to Europe. It just so happened that my parents were asked to teach a few courses (anthropology and phonetics) that summer in England as part of an SIL training session. So for several weeks, we lived at the Wycliffe Center in Horsleys Green, in the southeastern portion of England, known as Buckinghamshire. I remember very little of this time, but apparently, I adapted well as I was told that I had developed a rather accurate British accent. What I do remember, however, was the traveling we did on the way to my dad's teaching post in England with Granny and Grandpa Maree. Specifically, my grandfather wanted to take us to the places where he had fought in World War II.

I can remember traveling through Europe in a small (compact) white car—the make and model escape me—but I know it was small enough that, as a six-year-old, I felt cramped and squishy in the back seat next to my mother, sister, and grandmother. Back in those days, seat belts were not required, but even then, sitting as close as we could together, it was a miracle that we all managed to fit.

Grandpa had recently had an operation and was not allowed to drive, so my dad was responsible for driving us around Europe in a car with a right-side steering wheel on the left-side European roads. We managed like this starting out from England and traveling through the countries of Belgium, Luxembourg, France, Switzerland, and Italy, returning to England via Austria, Germany, and France. I can still picture (and smell) the apples we had purchased for a snack, baking in the hot sun under the back window of the car.

Knowing my affinity for motion sickness, we typically had a plastic bag (or several bags) at the ready. There was a time, however, when we somehow found ourselves without any bag. Upon our arrival in England and before we rented the small white car, Granny Maree had asked a cousin, whose husband was a chauffeur, to come pick us up at the airport and take us to where we would be spending the night. Apparently, we were on a stretch of road where pulling the car over was too difficult. Granny, calculated as she was, decided that it would be easier to clean out her purse than to pay to have the limousine cleaned! With lightning reflexes, she quickly opened her purse, and I emptied the contents of my stomach directly into it. I have no idea how many items from her purse she was able to salvage or how long it smelled like vomit, but I am grateful that only the contents of her purse were covered in my throw-up and not the entire back seat of the limousine!

This was "family bonding" at its finest. We toured what seemed like every castle in Europe, climbed the Leaning Tower of Pisa, and took pictures next to the bobbies at Buckingham Palace. I even sat on my dad's shoulders in the middle of the crowded streets of London and waved at Sarah Ferguson, the Duchess of York, as she made her way by carriage to Westminster Abbey for her wedding to Prince Andrew. Not only did we see the sites of Europe, but we also followed in Grandpa Maree's footsteps as he took us to the places he had fought during World War II.

We had all heard Grandpa's stories of "Betty," a lady who lived in Castiglione, Italy. She not only housed and fed my grandfather and his fellow soldiers but also helped to drag the wounded from piles of rubble. Together, she and my grandfather both saved and buried many soldiers and civilians.

To the best of my grandfather's recollection, he gave my dad directions, guiding him as he drove through various streets in the northern part of Italy. Amazingly, we not only found the village where Betty lived but also her home itself! Speaking only broken Italian, it took a while before my grandfather could explain to Betty, now a matronly grandmother, and her husband who he was. As Betty began to remember, the tears began to flow. She called for her daughter and son-in-law and her grandchildren to come, and together, she and my grandfather shared the story of how they had rescued so many in the middle of the war. Hours later, we were still in shock that we had found Betty and her family after so many years. Later, as we walked through the South African Cemetery in that area, I noticed my father weeping as my grandfather read the names on the white crosses. After each one, he would say, "*I buried him,*" or "*I knew him.*"

The culmination of our trip to Europe was in Dachau, Germany. This was one of the reasons we had come. Although my grandfather had fought on the front lines, making his way from northern Africa through Malta and Italy, he had never seen the atrocities of what had occurred in the concentration camps. I was only six years old, but my parents had explained to me the purpose of this concentration camp during the war. As we walked through Dachau, a feeling of horror filled me. Even now, it is difficult for me to write this as I remember seeing the wrought iron metalwork at the entrance to Dachau, the ovens, and the small, child-size jackets with yellow stars sewn on the front and back. We all wept as we made our way through the camp, knowing what evil had occurred there. Through tears, my grandfather whispered something along the lines of "*all that I had to do… it was worth it to stop this evil.*"

What we did not realize, however, was that this would not only be our last trip with Grandpa Maree, but it would also be one of the last times we would spend with him on this earth. And so, I am thankful to have had this time with Grandpa Maree. The last few days we spent with him and Granny Maree on our trip through Europe were very meaningful. He was gentle, kind, and a man who believed in the power of prayer. He called me his hummingbird. I am forever grateful to him and to the many thousands of others who fought so bravely and who even paid the ultimate sacrifice to end the horrors that occurred in places like Dachau.

I am also grateful for another family bonding experience that my family had many years later in China where we were able to experience more of my mother's heritage. During the summer of 1995, we met my uncle in Hong Kong for a special, two-week trip. This was an extraordinary vacation that allowed us to not only experience the sites of both Hong Kong and Macao but also to visit the original village where my grandparents (*Gung Gung* and *Pau Pau*) had lived in the province of Guangdong, China, before emigrating to the United States.

At the time of our visit, the ancestral home was still occupied by distant family relatives. It was impressive to see both my mother and my uncle switching with ease from English to Cantonese to Toisanese, a local dialect. Entering the traditional home where my grandparents had once lived, I noticed some familiar pictures on the wall. There were pictures of my immediate family and others of my mom's extended Ng family. I had heard stories of this village—the well outside the home and the rice fields surrounding the village. They were all still there. It was as if we had stepped back in time. This was a marvelous experience that provided me with a much better understanding of my mother's cultural heritage.

With all these international experiences and thrilling adventures, it is no wonder that I found a man who thrived on adventure as well. Kyle is no stranger to adventurous excursions. As a world traveler, he has not only experienced altitude sickness at Machu Picchu in Peru, snowboarded through the French Alps, climbed the iconic Sydney Harbour Bridge in Australia, and had emergency dental work done in Amsterdam, but he has also visited more than twenty countries and has lived in three.

During his initial trip to visit me in Canada in June of 2006, just a few months after we had met in Cambodia, we packed in as many activities as time would allow. We drove ATVs on a guided tour through the woods in Whistler, went skydiving in Abbotsford overlooking the beautiful Fraser Valley, and cliff jumped from forty-plus feet into glacier fed water in the UBC Research Forest in Maple Ridge. (We also experienced having my car broken into on Hastings Street in downtown Vancouver.)

By the time we had dated for a few years in Fort Worth, we had experienced many more exciting adventures together. While in Tanzania, on my first trip to Africa with MANNA Worldwide, Kyle let me know that he would be leaving Fort Worth for the Philippines on a work trip for two months on the same day that I would be returning to Fort Worth from Tanzania. After spending nearly one hundred dollars on a phone call to Kyle from the Amsterdam Airport, we were able to determine the exact time of my arrival in Minneapolis, as well as his exact departure. Our times would overlap by just a few hours. It was a miracle that our flight schedules coincided and that we were able to meet up with each other before our next flights, leaving me truly in awe of God's perfect timing.

Later that year, I was able to help lead another MANNA trip, this time to the island of Cebu in the

Philippines, where Kyle happened to be working at the time. Kyle joined us for the medical portion of the trip, helping screen patients by taking blood pressures and assisting the doctors and nurses with whatever needs they might have. He even arranged for our team to have a vacation day trip to tour the Chocolate Hills on the neighboring island of Bohol.

Panama was the next country that Kyle and I visited together while helping lead a MANNA youth trip. It was phenomenal to see the locks operating as a huge cargo ship went through the famous Panama Canal. What was even more impressive, however, was how Kyle once again threw himself into whatever task was required of him on this trip. He not only helped me and the other MANNA directors make sure all forty youths were on the bus each morning, but he was also typically seen on top of the bus, loading it with all the luggage from the team that wouldn't fit inside the bus. He played soccer with the Panamanian children, passed out food to the kids at the MANNA centers, and even painted a facility to be used for the MANNA church while experiencing a ferocious stomach bug.

The greatest adventure, however, was yet to begin. On the evening of February 24, 2009, Kyle asked me if I would share an adventure with him that would last our lifetime. Just like Comet Lulin that flashed through our skies in 2009, which would come around only once in our lifetime, he told me he didn't want to let me pass him by. Would I marry him? My answer was simple. A resounding "Yes!"

Perhaps one of our favorite movies is the first ten minutes of the 2009 Disney Pixar film *Up*. Carl and Ellie, adventurers for life, forged a bond of friendship during their early childhood years. As he is walking down the sidewalk one day, Carl hears a girl (Ellie) shouting, "*Adventure is out there!*" from the top of her lungs from somewhere inside her clubhouse. Curious, he steps inside and is introduced to a wild, redheaded, freckled little girl who dreams of adventure. Together, Carl and Ellie imagine exciting journeys on board the *Spirit of Adventure* blimp. Once married, they transform the run-down little clubhouse into their home of dreams and plan for a trip of a lifetime to Paradise Falls in Venezuela. Of course, as their married life unfolds, troubles come their way, and each time, their savings jar is emptied to pay for life's unfortunate circumstances. These setbacks don't seem to bother them, however, as they save up once again for another chance at Paradise Falls. Old age sets in, and Ellie eventually passes away. In his grief, Carl decides to take the entire clubhouse on one last adventure and finally visit Paradise Falls. The rest of the movie takes over after this, leading Carl on a completely different type of adventure than he ever imagined—an adventure that softens his wounded heart and opens his eyes to unexpected friendship.

Over the years, Kyle and I have watched and rewatched (with tears in our eyes) those first ten minutes of *Up*. I have realized that the adventure is not necessarily in the places we go or in the thrilling experiences we might have, but it is the journey we are experiencing together as we live life together. The greatest adventure is learning how to partner together so that our lives and our marriage reflect the love of Christ. As John Piper says,

> the deepest and highest meaning
> of marriage (is) not sexual intimacy,

> as good as that is, not friendship, or mutual helpfulness, or childbearing, or child-rearing, but the flesh-and-blood display in the world of the covenant-keeping love between Christ and his church.

The adventure is our life lived together, in what Piper says, is the *"radical call to faithfulness."*[121]

Paul David Tripp marvelously outlines marriage, saying that it is a *"gorgeous plan; in your marriage God will take you where you never thought you would go in order to give you what you could not achieve on your own."*[122] And so, Team O'Neal was established on October 10, 2009. Together, we face both life's joys and challenges. In faith, we step out together to experience the excitement of what God brings our way, trusting that He will guide us as we lean on Him. Together, we hold our hands high and shout at the top of our lungs from our own little clubhouse that we have built together, *"Adventure is out there!"*

---

[121] John Piper, *This Momentary Marriage* (Wheaton: Crossway Books, 2009), 175.

[122] Paul David Tripp, *What Did You Expect? Redeeming the Realities of Marriage* (Wheaton: Crossway Books, 2010), 217.

Thirteen

What the Locusts Ate

I will praise you, Lord my God, with all my heart; I will glorify your name forever. For great is your love toward me; you have delivered me from the depths.

Psalm 86:12–13a

"*I will repay you for the years the locusts have eaten.*"[123] Throughout my separation, divorce, and move to Texas, this was a verse that I clung to. I knew that God would never abandon me. I knew that He had a plan for my life, and I knew that I could trust Him. What I was unsure of was how long it would take for me to feel completely settled and at peace with where I was in life and who I was as His child.

I had times of doubt and seasons of discouragement when I felt I would never have the life I had always dreamed of. What I was beginning to learn during these difficult times was that my idea of the perfect life wasn't always what was best for me and that, even though God

---

[123] Joel 2:25 (NLT).

didn't reveal every step of His plan for my life at the time I wanted to see it, I could rest knowing that His promises are true. I could trust His Word and know that even though I couldn't see my future, I just needed to be faithful in where I was in my life and in what God had called me to do.

What exactly did the locusts eat? According to the prophet Joel, everything. "*The fields are ruined, the ground is dried up, the grain is destroyed, the new wine is dried up, the oil fails.*"[124] There was nothing left. The swarm of locusts consumed all that was green, all that could be used for food. There is a parallel in Joel's description of the army of locusts to the plague of locusts that covered the land of Egypt.[125] In both cases, it appears that the Lord is the one Who sent the locusts. In the book of Exodus, the Lord tells Moses to stretch out his hand over Egypt "*so that locusts will swarm over the land and devour everything growing in the fields, everything left by the hail.*"[126] The plague was so severe that it says, "*Never before had there been such a plague of locusts, nor will there ever be again.*"[127] The land was completely devastated, stripped bare. "*Nothing green remained on tree or plant in all the land of Egypt.*"[128]

Joel preaches to the nation of Israel, admonishing them to repent and return to the Lord because the day of the Lord's judgment is near. Clearly, however, the destruction that will occur by the locusts is carefully measured and is not unknown to the Lord. What stands out most

---

[124] Joel 1:10 (NLT).
[125] Joel 2:25.
[126] Exodus 10:12 (NLT).
[127] Exodus 10:14b (NLT).
[128] Exodus 10:15b (NIV).

to me is that the locusts and the total devastation they leave behind them are a direct result of sin. In the book of Exodus, the plague of locusts was sent as a punishment for Pharaoh's stubbornness in not allowing the people of Israel to leave. The locusts mentioned in the book of Joel foreshadow a day of crisis for the unrepenting nations, even Israel.

There are always consequences for sin. The effects can be immediate and can often be lingering, but regardless of when or how, Scripture is clear that there is always a penalty for sin. Paul says in the book of Romans that sin holds us as captives, binding us in slavery and condemning us to the ultimate penalty of death.[129] The death of a marriage certainly has far-reaching implications.

As I mourned the loss of my marriage, the broken covenant that was meant to last forever, I found myself in a state of bereavement. I felt that the fertile soil of my life had been eaten away by the locusts of sin and judgment. Divorce had stripped away not only my status as a married woman but also my dreams for a future. Would I ever be able to marry again or have a family? It felt as though there was nothing green left in my life. Even the soil of my heart felt dried and cracked, unable to even grow a weed.

As I dug into Scripture, I began to discover that even though I had a dream for my future, my greatest desire was to truly begin to know God and to genuinely desire what He wanted for my life. Nicki Koziarz expresses this so beautifully in her book *Why Her?*

---

[129] Romans 6:23 (NIV).

> When we humbly bring our desires and lay them alongside truth, we silence all the other voices that seek to influence us. And if what we desire doesn't line up with God's Word and character, we need to ask Him to help us see it...the closer we grow to Him, and the more we become like Him, the more we will only desire those things that more clearly reveal how our God is put on display through us.[130]

God's Word always shines truth, and for me, it provided comfort and reassurance that I was understood, loved, and cherished regardless of what I had experienced. *"Do you not know? Have you not heard? The Lord is the everlasting God, the Creator of the ends of the earth. He will not grow tired or weary, and his understanding no one can fathom."*[131] Surely, the God Who created the universe, Who created me, could understand the depths of my sorrow and the barrenness of the wilderness I was going through. As empty as I felt inside, I knew this was nothing compared to the anguish and abandonment my Lord must have felt on the cross, suffering for my sins. But because He conquered death and sin, because He rose victorious from the grave, I would also once again be restored. I knew I could cling to his Word, having confidence that even though I had been rejected and felt unloved, the Lord would never abandon me.

---

[130] Nicki Koziarz, Why Her?: 6 Truths We Need to Hear When Measuring Up Leaves Us Falling Behind (CITY: B&H Publishing Group, 2018), 130.

[131] Isaiah 40:29 (NLT).

> I have chosen you and have not rejected you. So do not fear, for I am with you; do not be dismayed, for I am your God. I will strengthen you and help you; I will uphold you with my righteous right hand... For I am the LORD, your God, who takes hold of your right hand and says to you, Do not fear; I will help you.[132]

Over and over again, I was reminded of God's promises in His Word. Even though my marriage had failed, I could trust that the Lord had a redemptive plan for my life. On May 9, 2001, when my marriage problems were just beginning, I wrote the words, *"You will restore me,"* in the margins of my Bible next to Isaiah 44:3, which says, *"For I will pour water on the thirsty land, and streams on the dry ground; I will pour out my Spirit on your offspring, and my blessing on your descendants."*[133] I claimed this verse as my own, just as I claimed the promise of children that the Lord showed me in my dream about the photo album. I clung to the hope that one day, my life would be restored and my hopes and dreams rejuvenated.

Isaiah 51:3 speaks of salvation for Zion, but I could trust that these promises were true for my life as well.

> The Lord will surely comfort [me] and will look with compassion on all [my] ruins; he will make [my] deserts like Eden, [my] waste-

---
[132] Isaiah 41:9b–10 (NLT).
[133] Isaiah 44:3 (NIV).

> lands like the garden of the LORD.
> Joy and gladness will be found in
> [me], thanksgiving and the sound of
> singing.[134]

Today's Christian culture has become relaxed in its view of the marriage covenant, and I want to be so careful that I do not convey a casual attitude toward the sacred and holy biblical view of marriage. There are certainly biblical scholars and theologians who hold fast to the view that there is no reason whatsoever that a divorced person is permitted to remarry while both partners are still alive. John Piper argues this point emphatically in his book, *This Momentary Marriage*. Because marriage is a picture of Christ and His bride, the church, Piper states that "*as long as Christ keeps his covenant with the church [and we know that God is faithful to fulfill his promises] and as long as the church, by the omnipotent grace of God, remains the chosen people of Christ, then the very meaning of marriage will include: What God has joined, only God can separate.*"[135] I wrestled with this particular argument as I contemplated divorce as well as my decision to remarry since I believe in the sacredness of marriage—that marriage binds two people together in a holy covenant that is mysterious and consecrated.

As I searched Scripture and sought the Lord for answers to my questions, I arrived at a place of peace. Numerous times, I had prayed through Psalm 80, underlining passages as I cried out to the Lord for restoration

---

[134] Isaiah 51:3 (NIV).
[135] John Piper, *This Momentary Marriage* (Wheaton: Crossway Books, 2009), 159.

and reconciliation for my marriage. *"Restore us, O God; make your face shine upon us, that we may be saved."*[136]

While Mathew 19:9 does allow for divorce because of marital unfaithfulness, it also clearly states that this was not God's intention for marriage. *"Moses permitted you to divorce your wives because your hearts were hard."*[137] All attempts at reconciliation with my ex-husband had failed. As far as I knew, there was no movement toward fidelity on his part. I then turned to Matthew 18:15–17, which outlines the steps that should be taken for confronting a brother in Christ who has sinned against you.

First, one should approach the believing brother privately, and if he will not listen, one or two others should come as witnesses. If reconciliation still does not happen after this, the matter should be brought to the church. I believe that after following these steps, without any resolution, I was able to confidently say that, with peace in my heart, I had been faithful to my marriage covenant.

Whichever position you take—the view that martial unfaithfulness is an exception granted for divorce or the position that there is never an exception that would allow for divorce—marriage is intended to be holy.

The redemptive work of Christ saves us from all sin and unrighteousness. While Romans 6:23 pronounces the judgment of sin as death, it also joyously declares with a resounding *but* that there is an alternative to death. The *"gift of God is eternal life through Christ Jesus our Lord."* While Piper is adamant that any remarriage after divorce (while the partner is still living) is adultery, he also points

---

[136] Psalm 80:3, 7, 19 (NIV).
[137] Matthew 19:8 (NIV).

to the generous forgiveness of Christ toward His bride, the church.

> The gospel of Christ crucified for our sins is the foundation of our lives. Marriage exists to display it. And when marriage breaks down, the gospel is there to forgive and heal and sustain until he comes, or until he calls.[138]

Ultimately, it is the redemptive work of Christ that is displayed in my life. I believe He saved me from sin and death through the power of His blood on the cross. The restorative work that was done in my life occurred out of the grace and goodness of Christ's love for me and *"so that people may see and know, may consider and understand, that the hand of the LORD has done this."*[139]

The day I said *"Yes"* to Kyle's marriage proposal was perhaps the happiest day of my life. Joy truly did flood my life and a garden of thankfulness began to grow within my heart. I believe the Lord, in His great compassion and mercy, granted my heart's desire to have a thriving marriage, a husband who seeks after the Lord with his whole heart, and two wonderful children who are a daily reminder of God's faithful, never-ending love for me. I know that the marriage I have today is sacred and holy.

Just as the Lord fulfilled his promise to Israel, I believe the Lord brought to fruition His promise to me

---

[138] John Piper, *This Momentary Marriage*, 175.
[139] Isaiah 41:20 (NLT).

in the dream He gave me so many years ago. *"I have loved you with an everlasting love, I have drawn you with loving-kindness. I will build you up again and you will be rebuilt."*[140] What the locusts of sin and divorce consumed in my life, the Lord replaced with blessings, both physically and spiritually, beyond what I could ever have imagined on my own.

After nearly three years of marriage, Kyle and I were beyond excited to meet the newest member of our family team. To add just a little bit of extra excitement and adventure to this wonderful and mysterious miracle of birth, we decided not to find out the gender of our precious little bundle. Somehow, we (and what seemed to be all our friends) were certain that it would be a boy! It seemed that O'Neals only produced boys. Kyle, being the middle of three boys, has no sisters, and his older brother and sister-in-law have been blessed with three boys. Even Kyle's younger brother has a son and no daughters.

On August 12, 2012, at four in the afternoon, Eden Maree O'Neal was born. She (yes, she!) was a perfectly healthy, beautiful little baby girl. Our joy was (and is) indescribable. Eden came a week early, on the day that Kyle completed a triathlon. While he was heroically displaying all types of manly athleticism, even cutting his foot coming out of the open water swim, unfortunately, his pain and the triumph of his successful finish were overshadowed by my labor and the arrival of a baby girl. At seven pounds and two ounces and twenty and quarter inches long, Eden completely, and rightfully so, stole the show and, of course, our hearts.

---

[140] Jeremiah 31:3–4a (NIV).

We named our little sweetie pie after the garden of Eden, a place that reveals the beauty and perfection of God's creativity, a place full of life and hope. We gave her my maiden name, Maree, as her middle name to carry on the Maree family name and because Kyle loved the name Marie (we just decided to spell it a little differently).

Today, Eden is the light of my heart and is growing into a beautiful, lovely young lady. Her determination and resolve are nearly unmatched. She is laser focused on her schoolwork, gymnastics routines, and list making, which finds her at the top of her class even though she is very often the youngest. When she smiles, my heart melts, and I know I will do anything and everything in my power to keep her safe.

At the age of four, she told us that she wanted to accept Jesus into her heart. This is the greatest gift that a parent could ever ask for! Through the years, and since that moment when I prayed with her to acknowledge not only her sinfulness but also the finished work of Christ on the cross for her, we have continued to see her grow in her knowledge and desire to follow Christ. Introspective and thoughtful, Eden often asks deeply provoking questions about how God created the world, why He is not a created being, and what heaven will look like. I love her inquisitive nature and the fact that she is searching for answers to so many mysteries that not even the greatest theologians can fully grasp.

I thought that my heart, full to the brim with love for both Kyle and sweet Eden, could not possibly have room for more when I found out I was pregnant again. Eden was barely six months old, yet I knew I had felt this unique type of miserable, nauseous feeling once before. (Did you know there are thirteen holes in a saltine cracker?) I was working full-time at two jobs and nursing an infant, so I was exhausted. At the same time, I was in a state of excitement and tremendous wonder that I was about to embark on another adventure. As with Eden, Kyle and I decided not to find out the gender of our second born. We recognized that there were so few true surprises in life, and we wanted to experience the thrill of the unknown one more time. This time, I was completely at a loss as to whether I thought my unborn baby would be a boy or a girl. I was secretly hoping for another girl because being raised in a house and dorm full of girls, I had absolutely no idea what I would do with a boy!

Early in the morning of October 21, 2013, three weeks before my due date, I begin to experience intense labor pains and bleeding. Calling Kyle's younger brother, who lived only a few minutes away, at four in the morning to come and watch Eden while we went to the hospital seemed a little surreal. Eden had just recently turned one and could barely even walk. She was also still quite attached to me and experienced separation anxiety that seemed to have started the moment she left my womb.

I can remember, when Eden was just a few weeks old, desperately wanting to take a shower. Passing a screaming infant into Kyle's arms, I would shower as quickly as possible, knowing Eden's sweet little face would be covered in hives from her incessant crying. The moment I took her back into my arms, she would stop crying, nestle into my chest, and immediately calm down. Years later, Eden still loves her mama!

Maverick Dean O'Neal was born a few hours after we got to the hospital, at seven in the morning. At six pounds and ten ounces and twenty inches long, he looked so tiny and frail, but I was absolutely enchanted.

Giving birth to Maverick without any pain medication or an epidural was like nothing I had ever experienced! I had asked for an epidural with Eden, but since my labor was so short (under two hours), she was born before it ever took effect. Because I knew that my labor would most likely also be short with my second baby, I decided to experience birth as naturally as I could. I'm not sure who was more surprised at the strength of my lungs as I screamed in pain, my husband or me! I would never trade the experience, however, and am so grateful that I was able to deliver two healthy babies.

Maverick has certainly lived up to his name. He is rowdy and rambunctious, full of fun, witty, inquisitive, and genuinely happy-go-lucky. Just like his sister, we found that gymnastics was a natural sport for him. It not only allowed him to grow into one of the strongest kids that I know, but it also provided him with an opportunity to burn off all the energy he had! We gave him the name Maverick because it is a strong name—the name of a leader, of a trailblazer. Dean is my father's middle name. And so, both of my children are truly a blend, a merging of both the O'Neal and Maree families. They are also both children of God.

At five years old, Maverick announced that he wanted to have Jesus in his heart. When I asked him to pray the prayer of salvation with me, he told me, *"Mom, I've already prayed that prayer for Jesus to come into my heart!"* My heart still bursts with joy!

> I praise you, Father, Lord of heaven and earth, because you have hidden these things from the wise and learned, and revealed them to lit-

tle children. Yes, Father, for this was
your good pleasure.[141]

I want to be careful here. If you were to just read these last few paragraphs, it would sound like my life was perfect. You might find yourself saying, *"She got everything she wanted. She got the guy, the kids, the adventure of a lifetime."* Yes, there is truth in that statement. I did get "the guy" and "the kids" and "the adventure of a lifetime." I did get the fulfillment of a dream, and because of that, I do have the photo album with pictures of birthday parties and family adventures, but I still carry the scars from the battle wounds that you may have forgotten about at the beginning of this chapter, or perhaps from chapter 8. And this is not to say that there won't be sorrow, disappointment, and failure in my future. My point is this: Please do not read this book and begin to compare your life, whether there are triumphs or trials, to the experiences I have chosen to record in this book. There are many, many incidents, both joyful and painful, that I chose to leave out. The purpose of recording these memories is not to compare my life with someone else's but to point both myself and you, as the reader, to God's faithfulness through both the failures and the victories.

There is nothing that I did in my life to deserve the blessings, or perhaps even some of the sorrows that I have experienced. Scripture is very clear that the Lord never promises to give us a life without the burden of pain and suffering. What He did promise, however, is that He would never leave us and that, if we put our hope and our trust in Him, we would experience a peace that

---
[141] Matthew 11:25–26 (NIV).

passes all understanding.[142] In her book *Why Her?*, Nicki Koziarz reminds us that

> comparison's lie of lack would love for both of us to believe that the other's gift is more important, more significant, more special, that what the other person gains by exercising her gifts, we somehow lose.

In short, she says that when you make comparisons, remember that

> her gain is not your loss...it's easy to assume the best things are taken, and that there's nothing good left for us. But this lie of lack leaves us missing what's right in front of us.[143]

If we truly believe that God has a good plan for our lives,[144] then we simply cannot waste precious time comparing what we see as a lack of blessings in our lives to what we assume is an overabundance of blessings in the lives of others. All I can do is declare the goodness of the Lord in my life, both in my sufferings when the locusts are laying waste to my dreams and in my rejoicings when peace and gladness reign. Truly, my heart can say, *"I will tell of the kindness of the LORD, the deeds for which he is to be praised, according to all the LORD has done for us."*[145]

---

[142] Philippians 4:7 (NIV).
[143] Nicki Koziarz, *Why Her?*, 155–156.
[144] Jeremiah 29:11.
[145] Isaiah 63:7 (NIV).

The other point I want to make is that while we may have times in our life when the locusts swarm and devour every good thing, we must trust that the Lord and Creator of the universe still holds us in His hands. We must acknowledge the desert, the barrenness, and the anguish, but instead of lamenting what the locusts have consumed, we *"fix our eyes on Jesus."*[146] Our only hope comes through the resurrected power of Christ. Jesus Christ faced the blackness of sin and death and rose victorious over the grave, and because of that we, too, can claim victory over the darkness and devastation in our lives.

> Surely the arm of the Lord is not too short to save, nor his ear too dull to hear[147] [because] in all their distress he too was distressed, and the angel of his presence saved them. In his love and mercy he redeemed them; he lifted them up and carried them all the days of old.[148]

David says in Psalm 40,

> I waited patiently for the Lord to help me, and he turned to me and heard my cry. HE lifted me out of the pit of despair, out of the mud and the mire. He set my feet on solid ground and steadied me as I walked

---

[146] Hebrews 12:2 (NIV).
[147] Isaiah 59:1 (NIV).
[148] Isaiah 63:9 (NIV).

> along. HE has given me a new song to sing, a hymn of praise to our God. Many will see what he has done and be amazed. They will put their trust in the Lord.[149]

And if redemption doesn't come in the way that we envision it, we can say with confidence that

> though the fig tree does not bud and there are no grapes on the vines, though the olive crop fails and the fields produce no food, though there are no sheep in the pen and no cattle in the stalls, yet I will rejoice in the Lord, I will be joyful in God my Savior. The Sovereign LORD is my strength.[150]

This is my prayer for you. This is my prayer for me: that I will continually turn my face to seek the Lord and that I will acknowledge Him as my Lord and my Savior, regardless of whether I live in plenty or if I live in sorrow. For He bore the greatest sorrow of all, and because of His anguish, I am redeemed.

---

[149] Psalm 40:1–3 (NIV).
[150] Habakkuk 3:17–19a (NIV).

Fourteen

To Run and Not Grow Weary

And let us run with perseverance the race marked out for us, fixing our eyes on Jesus, the author and perfecter of our faith.

Hebrews 12:1b–2a

My move to Texas was difficult, but over time, I began to find my groove with work and friends. I also found a church to call home and joined a ladies' Bible study group. As I began to settle into life in Texas, I realized that for me to feel at home in my new surroundings, I would need to incorporate some things that I really enjoyed back into my life—things that made my heart full.

One of those "things" was physical exercise. I had always enjoyed running, but I had never really run with intentionality before, other than to just enjoy the outdoors and stay in shape. After my move to Texas, I decided that I could run with more purpose.

Playing the piano was another one of those "things." I was teaching quite a bit, even before Kyle and I were married, but I hadn't really been playing pieces that challenged me or made me feel like I was progressing in my own abilities as a musician.

Not long before Kyle proposed to me, I decided to once again take the ARCT Piano Performer's Exam through the Royal Conservatory of Music, Toronto. I had previously completed all the theory requirements for the degree and now just needed to pass the practical portion of the exam that I had originally failed while living in Canada. Of course, the fear of failing a second time lurked in the back of my mind, but I was determined that this time would be different. The fact that I didn't own a piano didn't bother me. Hallmark Baptist Church was gracious enough to let me use their piano to practice. And so, before work in the morning, I would practice for a few hours around 6:30 or 7:00 a.m., and then after work in the evening, I would let myself into the church and practice for a few more hours until around eleven at night or even until midnight some nights. (Incidentally, on the way home from one of these late-night practices, I received my first speeding ticket because I was so tired and anxious to get home to bed. The police officer was a little skeptical that a young lady in her twenties was really coming from a piano practice session at midnight!)

After over a year of lessons and too many hours of practicing to even begin to count, the day for my piano exam came. I was too nervous to drive the hour and a half it would take to get to Plano, Texas, where my exam was being held, so Kyle drove me. Little did I know that he had purchased flowers to give to me from my parents after I had finished playing my exam and, for the icing on the cake, had arranged for us to go bungee jumping to celebrate the completion of my exam. I was ecstatic!

With the weight of the exam behind me, bungee jumping was the perfect way to celebrate and release all the adrenaline and tension that had crept up on me during the exam.

I know my parents and possibly a myriad of others will not agree with me, but this was a fantastic way to celebrate! I enjoyed the experience so much that for my fortieth birthday, I asked Kyle to take me bungee jumping again! The second time we went, we also added in the zero gravity drop, which was even more adrenaline boosting. I will admit, however, that at forty, my bungee-jumping experience was a little different from the bungee-jumping experience I had in my twenties. I not only experienced a little bit of actual terror but also nausea and perhaps even some vertigo afterward. (It was still worth it, in my opinion, but my mother will be happy to hear me say that I have now sufficiently had my fill of bungee jumping, at least for now, and the chances of me declining the next time bungee jumping is offered have now been increased to at least 50 percent!)

The real cause for celebration, however, came a few weeks later when I discovered that I had passed my piano exam! I thought back to the moment just four years prior when I had received the news that I had failed. God had been faithful to me these last four years, healing me, teaching me, guiding me, and all the while never leaving me. With this second opportunity to take the exam, I was filled with an overwhelming sense of joy and gratitude.

Psalm 33 is a song of rejoicing, a declaration of the Lord's goodness and faithfulness, and this time, from deep within my heart, I was able to sing along with the psalmist, praising God for his kindness to me.

> Sing joyfully to the Lord, you righteous; it is fitting for the upright to praise him...Sing to him a new song; play skillfully, and shout for joy. For the word of the Lord is right and true; he is faithful in all he does.[151]

I felt not only a sense of accomplishment but also absolute relief because, in many ways, having passed that exam released me from any negative ties to the past. With a piano performer's degree in my hands, I could start fresh. No looking back.

The discipline of preparing for a piano exam also taught me many things about my own character. Practicing for such a monumental performance is like training for a marathon. Both require patience, perseverance, endurance, determination, long hours of practice, and a whole lot of prayer. Just as memorizing a Beethoven piano sonata is not going to happen in a week or even after several months, a marathon is not going to happen quickly. As the pressure of my piano exam faded into the distance, I began to focus on other areas of my life.

I have always enjoyed running. I'm not sure exactly what the initial attraction was, but perhaps it was because it did not require any fancy equipment or demand perfect vision. Running can be done in groups or solo, in just about any weather, and at any pace. Running takes you outside into nature, allowing you to process what you see in somewhat slow motion, instead of letting it fly by your car window as you drive.

---

[151] Psalm 33:1, 3–4 (NIV).

Kyle and I began to sign up for a few 5Ks. It was nothing too demanding, but a challenge nonetheless. The goal, at least for me, was to make what I had paid for the race worthwhile by at least crossing the finish line in a respectable amount of time. Kyle, of course, being the athlete that he is, was always way ahead of me, had typically already received his finisher medal, and was waiting at the finish line for me to cross by the time I hit mile three. But that didn't really bother me. As a self-motivator, I was mostly interested in just beating my own time.

The more races we ran, the more adventurous we became in our running. Probably the most challenging and exciting 5K we ran, in my opinion, was the Warrior Dash in Forney, Texas. There were several obstacles on the 3.1-mile course, including running through a rocky riverbed, scrambling over large bales of hay (while wet, muddy, and sticky), swimming over and under humungous tree logs floating in a river, and army crawling through mud underneath barbed wire. Exhilarating! Exhausted, soaking wet, and covered in mud and grime, I crossed the finish line with a sense of accomplishment.

As 5Ks turned into 10Ks, we discovered that running a half-marathon was an attainable goal to strive for. Each year, the running of the Cowtown Marathon occurs in Fort Worth during the last weekend of February. After running both the 5K and the 10K in the Cowtown, Kyle and I decided that the half-marathon was a worthy goal to pursue. Over a decade later, we are still running the Cowtown half-marathon race each year. I look forward to every fall when we begin training, not only because the weather is cooler and running longer distances becomes more enjoyable but also because of the thrill and excitement of running in a large race.

Nearly thirty thousand people run the various events (5K, 10K, half-marathon, marathon, and ultra-marathon) over two days. That's a lot of people! Not to mention the bystanders, support staff, and volunteers throughout the course. It's exhilarating to run alongside so many other runners through the streets of your own city, being cheered on by complete strangers who have lined the streets to wave, hold banners, man the hydration stations, and pass out food.

There are even several bands stationed along the course providing music to boost the morale of the runners as they dig deep to complete their respective races.

One day, Kyle informed me that he would like to run a full marathon. While I knew he could certainly complete it, I was in awe at the very thought of someone I knew who would soon be a marathoner. As he began his training, I started to realize the monumental goal he was undertaking. The marathon itself was really the culmination of several months of training, running thirty-five to forty miles every week. While the training is a feat in itself, at the time, we had two children under the age of two. Some days, it seemed that the greatest effort was to get out of bed and go to work, never mind running that many miles over seven days.

On the day of his big race, we woke up early, at 5:00 a.m., to prepare. Although Maverick was only four months old at the time, I had decided to run the half-marathon that year. This is the only race that Kyle and I have run together, side by side, at least for the first ten miles before the marathoners split off to continue the rest of their race. After crossing the finish line, I hurried home to shower; meet Pam, my mother-in-law, who was watching our children; feed Maverick; and then hurry back to cheer on Kyle as he crossed the finish line and completed his first marathon. What an accomplishment! I was bursting with pride for Kyle!

The fact that Kyle had trained and run a full marathon got me thinking, *Maybe I can do one too?* I began training, and within a few months, I decided to sign up for the Fort Worth Marathon, which would take place that November. I somehow managed to find time to train between working for MANNA, teaching piano, taking care of two small children, and spending quality time with family. Truly, my only goal was to finish the race, which thankfully, I did! As I crossed the finish line, I remember thinking that I never wanted to do this again! I should have remembered what I learned in elementary school: that you "never say never" because, six years later, in 2020, I ran the full marathon, and then in 2024 I competed the ultra marathon!

Our children have now caught the running bug and have completed several 5K races of their own. It's been a tremendous joy to be able to run alongside my children and cross the finish line together. Father Patrick Peyton is credited with coining the catchphrase, "A family that prays together stays together." While that can certainly be true, I have, in jest, adapted the slogan for fitness purposes: "A family that runs together stays fit together!"

All joking aside, physical fitness has always been a priority for Kyle and me, so it is natural that our children have adopted that mindset as well. There is, however, no shortage of nacho chips, sour candy, or ice cream at our house. We eat all carbs and are regular partakers of chocolate chip cookies, pasta, and chicken potpie. On the other hand, I can hardly contain the pride I feel when my children turn down a cupcake because it is too sweet or order a salad for dinner at a restaurant. As my mother would frequently tell me growing up, *"Everything in moderation."* (Hopefully, one day, my children will remember any words of wisdom I had and will choose to quote me! Thanks, Mom!)

Teaching our children what healthy, balanced living looks like is a challenge. It takes patience, discernment, perseverance, love, and gentleness. While they have certainly started their own journey toward physical fitness, working to achieve their own goals, music has also become a big part of their lives. As a piano teacher, I would be doing my children a disservice if I didn't at least teach them how to read music. I will admit that the thought did cross my mind: *What if I am not able to teach my children the basic musical concepts that I am able to teach other children?* I am happy to report that both my children are still enrolled in music lessons with me, are making progress, and even enjoy playing the piano! I am beyond thrilled that my children are learning to read music and appreciate the discipline it takes to practice and learn their pieces.

I have discovered that raising children is also like preparing for a piano exam or training for a marathon, particularly when it comes to the area of patience and endurance! When Eden and Maverick were infants, my first goal as a new mother was to literally keep them alive! Of course, I knew the ultimate goal was to raise them in a loving Christian home, but in reality, as much as I loved them, I felt as though, practically, I had no idea what I was doing! I'm sure most new mothers can relate to the postpartum feelings I had, fearful that I would somehow fail in these most basic of human instincts. The other practical aspects of motherhood, like making sure they had clean diapers on, somehow getting the dirty laundry washed, and then putting dinner on the table, were overwhelming tasks, but they needed to be done. I felt as if I was in survival mode.

During those early years with two children under the age of two, the number of dirty diapers and laundry that those two sweet babies created was literally mind-blowing! They either seemed to take a large, rather explosive poop at the same time or one right after the other. It's like they planned it, plotting and scheming to see what would cause me the most distress.

I can remember one incident when both children were in the throes of potty training. Maverick was nearing two years old, and Eden was about to turn three. Both children were happily playing in Eden's room while I was unloading the dishwasher. I heard Eden's frantic scream and came running. What I saw produced both hysterical laughter and immediate stress. The scene will forever be burned in my mind. Eden was huddled in the furthest corner of her toddler bed, pointing at Maverick and screaming at the top of her lungs. Maverick, who seemed to be oblivious to the distress he was causing his sister, was naked from the waist down and was in a squatted position inside his toy dump truck, his bare rear end hanging over the end of the dump truck. A pile of fresh poop sat directly under his naked bum. While I wasn't quick enough to get a picture of the entire scene before Maverick jumped off the dump truck, I did manage to take a picture of his poop and sent it to his father at work. My caption read something along the lines of *"Aren't you glad you are at work today?"*

What I discovered, far too late, was that not everything needed to be accomplished every day for me to feel like I had crossed the finish line. I was so determined to finish my daily race, having completed a respectable number of tasks, and then swiftly and gracefully cross the finish line with a smile on my face at the end of the day that sometimes I needed a good, hilarious "dump" event to snap me out of my task-oriented day. The reality was that, most nights, I was barely able to crawl over the finish line, certainly not in a very graceful manner, and my smile was weak at best. Incidents like the dump truck and the poop on Eden's bedroom carpet are things that we laugh about today as a family. "*Maverick, can you believe you did that?*" "*Eden, can you believe Maverick pooped on your carpet?*" The kids still think it is hilarious and often ask me to pull up the picture of Maverick's poop on my phone.

As my children grew, became potty-trained (no more poop on the carpet!), and learned how to feed and dress themselves, life became a lot less hectic. Not having to change so many diapers (or purchase them) was a milestone worthy of celebration! Before we knew it, Kyle and I found ourselves moving from survival mode to disciplining and discipling. We discovered that the goal was more than simply keeping them alive! It was more about nurturing our children and raising them to know and love the Lord. We began to ask ourselves, *How do we disciple our children to become not simply productive members of society but also vibrant, whole-hearted followers of Christ?* We still ask ourselves that question every day, since we have been entrusted to care for Eden and Maverick for such a short period of time.

Psalm 127 says that children are a *"gift from the Lord; they are a reward from him."*[152] Discipling them and teaching them to truly know the Lord and live a life of service in gratitude for His completed work on the cross should be the goal of every Christian parent. I am teaching my children to understand that just as it takes time to learn to play the piano or to build up endurance to run a 5K, it takes time to learn and grow in your relationship with Jesus. Because both Eden and Maverick have professed their faith in Jesus Christ and have declared their desire to follow Him, they are both in the process of sanctification, of daily becoming more and more like Jesus. I am glad that they share our love for music, the outdoors, and physical activity, but more importantly, I am excited they are learning that all their talents and abilities come from the Lord.

> Every good and perfect gift is from above, coming down from the Father of the heavenly lights, who does not change like shifting shadows. He chose to give us birth through the word of truth, that we might have a kind of firstfruits of all he created.[153]

Just as in other areas of life, parenting has revealed opportunities for both failure and victory. As a human, marred by sin and scarred by the pain and hurts the world has offered, I will be the first to admit that I have failed

---

[152] Psalm 127:3 (NIV).
[153] James 1:17 (NIV).

as a parent. I have raised my voice, lost my patience, and spoken with unkindness and anger. And yet, there is grace. I know that I am redeemed and forgiven, but more than that, I continue to be whittled down, sharpened and refined, my rough edges smoothed, and my heart purified so that I am, in incremental ways, becoming more like my Father in heaven. Therein lies the beauty.

"*Therefore, we do not lose heart. Though outwardly we are wasting away, yet inwardly we are being renewed day by day. For our light and momentary troubles are achieving for us an eternal glory that far outweighs them all.*"[154] What a blessed hope! Our failures are not remembered. In this marathon of life, we are certain to have difficulties, trials, disappointments, hurts, fears, uncertainties, and long, exhausting days—days when we question our parenting and have doubts about our abilities. And yet, when we "*fix our eyes not on what is seen, but on what is unseen,*" our focus shifts from the temporal to the eternal.[155]

Failure, disappointment, and heartache are inevitable. We cannot go through life without experiencing pain in some form. And yet, as we remember the anguish and sorrow that Christ endured on the cross for us, we can live our lives with joy, knowing that our distress will not last forever. Because of this, "*let us strip off every weight that slows us down, especially the sin that so easily trips us up. And let us run with endurance the race God has set before us. We do this by keeping our eyes on Jesus, the champion who initiates and perfects our faith.*"[156]

Whether it's preparing for a final piano exam, training for a marathon, raising children, or juggling the daily

---

[154] 2 Corinthians 4:16–17 (NIV).
[155] 2 Corinthians 4:8 (NIV).
[156] Hebrew 12:1b–2 (NLT).

tasks life requires, we know that, as we put our trust and eternal hope in the Lord, He will daily renew our strength. He will lift us up on an eagle's wings so that we can soar above the weight and darkness of sin and death. We will *"run and not grow weary,"*[157] our eyes fixed on Jesus until we cross the final finish line.

Dear friend, have hope. Cling to the eternal promise of victory over sin, death, fear, and trials. Know that you are not alone. You are immeasurably loved and sought-after.

---

[157] Isaiah 40:31 (NIV).

I will sing to the Lord all my life; I will sing praise to you God as long as I live.

Psalm 104:33

Photos

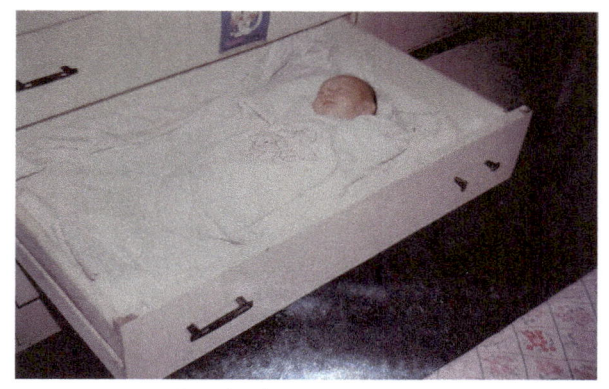

My first bed: SIL Guest House,
Manila, Philippines,
January 20–23, 1980

In front of our family home on Babuyan Island:
August 1980

© WorldAtlas.com
Balintang Channel
Babuyan Island
Cabaroan
Banua
Calayan Island
Pacific Ocean
South China Sea
Calayan
Dalupiri Island
Babuyan Islands
Philippine Sea
Fuga Island
Poso
PHILIPPINES
Camiguin Island
Babuyan Channel
N
Palaui Island
20 m
20 km
Aparri
Luzon Island

Going to the *Oksong* (spring) to wash clothes and do the dishes: Babuyan 1983

Roots and wings picture in our house on Babuyan

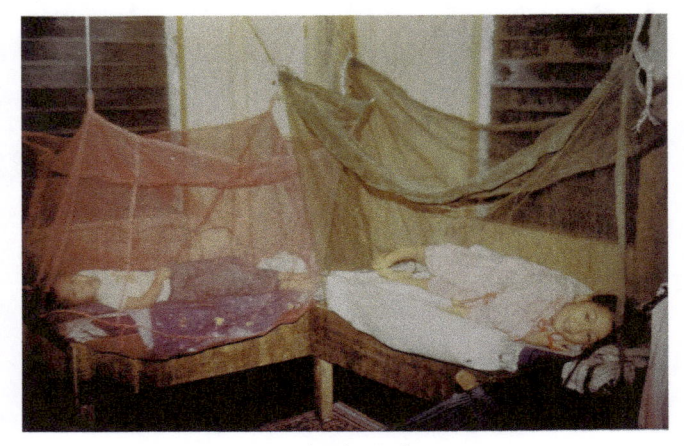

Corner beds: Babuyan
1982

Balcony of our family home on Babuyan Island, Philippines:
September 1987

What was left of our house on
Babuyan after typhoon *Pepang:*
October 23, 1987

RP43: Leaving Babuyan after *Pepang:*
October 1987

New cement and lava rock house on
Babuyan after typhoon *Pepang*:
1989

Washing clothes at the *Oksong*: Babuyan,
December 1989

Third airstrip on Babuyan at sea level:
1987

Family climbing expedition, *Chinteb a Wasay,* Babuyan
1995

Family climbing expedition, *Pokis:* Babuyan
1996

Our family home at the SIL Center in Bagabag, Philippines:
1987

Bagabag

Early days of piano practice with a small
battery-operated keyboard:
July 1985

Bagabag Elementary/middle school (K–8):
1986

New Year's Day in Bagabag:
January 1, 1981

Motorcycle accident:
January 27, 1985

226 | IS THERE ANYTHING IN THE CORNER?

Ng family in San Francisco:
December 1984

Maree family in Ladysmith, British Columbia, Canada:
1981

Nasuli Spring, Mindanao, Philippines: Baptism,
June 24, 1990

Flute ensemble, Fort Langley, British Columbia, Canada:
1993

High school physics students holding flags on the
roof. Tami: Eighth from the left, holding Canadian
flag; Faith Academy, Manila, Philippines:
1997

Playing with the children at the MANNA center in
Mombasa, Kenya:
2007

Kyle and Tami with the children at the
MANNA center in Nairobi, Kenya:
2010

O'Neal family
2023

Acknowledgments

It is quite impossible to name all the people who encouraged me to write this book (but I'll try!). Each one of these individuals helped give me the confidence to put my story on paper, even when I felt I didn't have a story to tell, and for that, I am thankful.

Tiffany, you were the first person to read my story (unedited as it was!). Thank you for being my sounding board.

Rebecca, I have much to learn from you about the art of writing. Thank you for being willing to take a chance on me and for challenging me to dig a little deeper.

To my parents, thank you for teaching me the value of hard work and the importance of family. I am most thankful to you, however, for not only introducing me to Jesus but also for modeling what it means to be a Christ follower. Thank you for the sacrifices you made for our family growing up. And thank you for reading this book in its entirety, commenting, editing, and polishing my writing.

Bruce and Pam, thank you for welcoming me into your family and for unconditionally opening your home and your hearts to me.

Kyle, my husband, my friend, my confidant, my biggest supporter—you are someone I can't imagine my life without. Thank you for listening to me, for seeing me, and for understanding me (at least for trying to!). Thank you for challenging me to pursue my dreams and for standing by me to cheer me on in the process. Thank you for choosing me and for creating Team O'Neal with me. I am so grateful to be living this life of adventure with you!

To Eden and Maverick, you fill my heart with joy! Thank you for teaching me to see the wonder in the mundane and for inspiring me each day with your laughter and curiosity. Our life together is my dream come true, and I thank God each day for the privilege of being your mom. "I love you forever!"

I am so grateful for the people whom God brought into my life to help shape me and sharpen me. Thank you to my friends and family for your love and support: Marlaena, Corrie, Natasha, Maia, Chuck and Patty, Bill and Carey, Aunt Carol and Jennifer (many of whom are already mentioned in the pages of the book). Thank you, Molly, for encouraging me to publish this. Beth, Charlie and Ashleigh, Hailey, Taylor, MC, Mary, Kristen, and Darlene—thank you for your persistence in asking me how my writing was coming along, for deep and meaningful conversations, for encouraging me in my faith, and for being willing to call me a friend. Charlie, thank you also for the beautiful cover design! You have a gift for creativity, and I am so very thankful for your willingness to help me transform my thoughts into art!

To all those who have contributed to the various events in my life and who have had an impact on me throughout my growing-up years, thank you. My life is what it is because of the circumstances I have experienced. And yet, my life is significantly more than the sum of a series of events and episodes strung together for the entertainment of others. I have life because Jesus breathed life into my soul. His death on the cross set me free from the chains of sin and sorrow. His victory over death grants me life eternal in His very presence. My story is simply this: *"Come and hear, all you who fear God; let me tell you what he has done for me"* (Psalm 66:16).

Bibliography

Big Daddy Weave. "Redeemed."Track #7 on *Love Come to Life*. Curb Records/Fervent Records, 2012.

Doerksen, Brian. "Creation Calls." Track #10 on *Today*. Hosanna! Music, 2004. Compact disc.

Ferrer, Hillary Morgan. General Editor. *Mama Bear Apologetics: Empowering Your Kids to Challenge Cultural Lies*. Harvest House Publishers, 2019.

Foster, Richard. *Prayer: Finding the Heart's True Home*. HarperOne, 2003.

Kent, Carol. *Becoming a Woman of Influence*. NavPress, 2006.

Koziarz, Nicki. *Why Her? 6 Truths We Need to Hear When Measuring Up Leaves Us Falling Behind*. B&H Publishing Group, 2018.

Layton, Tasha. "Look What You've Done." Track #7 on *How Far*. BEC Recordings, 2022.

Lewis, C. S. *Mere Christianity*. HarperCollins Publishers, 1952.

Lucado, Max. *In the Grip of Grace: You Can't Fall Beyond His Love*. W Publishing Group, 1996.

Manning, Brennan. *The Rabbi's Heartbeat*. NavPress, 2003.

Maree, Judith. "*Pepang,*" Personal Journal Entry. November 1987.

Merriam-Webster Dictionary. "Determination." Accessed August 20, 2021. https://www.merriam-webster.com/dictionary/determination.

Montgomery, L. M. *Anne of Green Gables.* Seal Books, 1996.

Piper, John. *This Momentary Marriage: A Parable of Permanence.* Crossway, 2012.

Stuckey, Allie Beth. *You're Not Enough (And That's Okay): Escaping the Toxic Culture of Self-Love.* Penguin Random House, 2020.

The Bible. New Living Translation.

The Bible. New International Version.

Patrick, John. *The Curious Savage.*

The Princess Bride. Directed by Rob Reiner, 20th Century Fox, 1987.

Tolkien, J. R. R. 1892–1973. *The Hobbit, Or, There and Back Again.* Authorized ed., Rev. ed. London: HarperCollins Publishers, 1999. Print.

Tripp, Paul David. *What Did You Expect?: Redeeming the Realities of Marriage.* Crossway, 2009.

U2. "Sweetest Thing." Track #8 on *The Best of U2 1980–1990.* Island Records, 1998. Compact disc.

Up. Directed by Pete Docter and Bob Peterson, Walt Disney Pictures, 2009.

Maps

World Atlas. "Babuyan Islands." Last modified 2024. https://www.worldatlas.com/islands/babuyan-islands.html.

Wikipedia. "Bagabag, Nueva Vizcaya." Last modified November 15, 2023. https://en.wikipedia.org/wiki/Bagabag,_Nueva_Vizcaya.

About the Author

Tami was born in the Philippines and lived most of her growing-up years as a missionary kid in the northern part of the country. After leaving the Philippines in her late teens, she spent nearly a decade living in British Columbia, Canada. She is an alumna of Trinity Western University and The Royal Conservatory of Music. Tami now makes her home in Fort Worth, Texas, with her husband, Kyle, and her two children, Eden and Maverick.

She and her husband love their church and are deeply involved as volunteers. Tami is the founder and owner of O'Neal Music Studio, where she teaches piano to students of all ages. While music is a big part of her everyday life, you can often find her running on the trails, reading a good book, or hanging out with her family. She loves to try new foods, particularly anything that is spicy, and her favorite dessert is chocolate cake. Tami's desire is to embrace the adventure of living her God-given life to the fullest. Regardless of circumstances or past experiences, her heart is for every individual to live life with open arms, to receive grace, and to truly experience the depths of God's eternal faithfulness and love.